HAPPINESS IN THIS LIFE

POPE FRANCIS

Happiness in This Life

A Passionate Meditation on
Material Existence and the Meaning of Life

Edited by
NATALE BENAZZI

Translated from the Italian by
SHAUN WHITESIDE

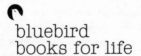

bluebird
books for life

This edition first published in the UK 2018 by Bluebird
an imprint of Pan Macmillan
20 New Wharf Road, London N1 9RR
Associated companies throughout the world
www.panmacmillan.com

ISBN 978-1-5098-8650-0

La Felicità in Questa Vita
by Jorge Mario Bergoglio, Papa Francesco
© 2017 – Libreria Editrice Vaticana, Città del Vaticano
© 2017 – EDIZIONI PIEMME Spa, Milano
www.edizpiemme.it

Translation by Shaun Whiteside

1 3 5 7 9 8 6 4 2

A CIP catalogue record for this book is available from the British Library.

Typeset by Palimpsest Book Production Ltd, Falkirk, Stirlingshire
Printed and bound by CPI Group (UK) Ltd, Croydon, CR0 4YY

Visit *www.panmacmillan.com* to read more about all our books
and to buy them. You will also find features, author interviews and
news of any author events, and you can sign up for e-newsletters
so that you're always first to hear about our new releases.

CONTENTS

THE PATH OF HAPPINESS

The Beatitudes are the road that God indicates as an answer to man's innate desire for happiness, and they perfect the commandments of the Old Testament. We are used to learning the Ten Commandments – of course you all know them, you learned them in religious instruction – but we are not used to repeating the Beatitudes. Let's try to remember them and imprint them in our hearts.

First: 'Blessed are the poor in spirit, for theirs is the kingdom of heaven.

'Blessed are those who mourn, for they will be comforted.

'Blessed are the meek, because they will inherit the earth.

'Blessed are those who hunger and thirst for righteousness, for they will be filled.

'Blessed are the merciful, for they will be shown mercy.

'Blessed are the pure in heart, for they will see God.

'Blessed are the peacemakers, for they will be called children of God.

'Blessed are those who are persecuted because of righteousness, for theirs is the kingdom of heaven.

'Blessed are you when people insult you, persecute you and falsely say all kinds of evil against you because of me.

'Rejoice and be glad, because great is your reward in heaven.'

Pick up the Gospel, the one you carry with you . . . Remember that you must always carry a little Gospel with you, in your pocket, in your handbag, always. The Beatitudes are in Matthew Chapter 5. Read them every day so that you don't forget them, because they are the Law that Jesus gives us!

These words contain the whole of the news brought by Christ, and all the news of Christ is in those words. In fact, the Beatitudes are the portrait of Jesus, his form of life; and they are the path towards happiness, which we too can travel with the grace that Jesus gives us.

General audience, 6 August 2014

PART I

YOUR LIFE
IN SEARCH OF
MEANING

DREAMS AND PLANS,
THE FUTURE AND HOPE

'With Jesus Christ
joy is always born and reborn'
Evangelii gaudium

———

The Gospel of the fulfilled life

The joy of the Gospel fills the heart and the whole life of those who encounter Jesus. Those who allow themselves to be saved by him are freed from sin, from sadness, from inner emptiness, from isolation.

Evangelii gaudium, 1

———

The big question: is hope possible, here and now?

The dizzying rhythm that we are subjected to seems to rob us of hope and joy. Pressures and powerlessness in the face of many situations seem to dry up our souls and make us insensitive to countless challenges. And paradoxically, when everything is speeding up to build – in theory – a better society, in the end we have no time for anything or anybody. We lose time for family, time for community, we lose time for friendship, for solidarity and for memory.

We should ask ourselves: *how is it possible to experience the joy of the Gospel today within our cities? Is Christian hope possible in this situation, here and now?*

These two questions touch our identity, the lives of our families, of our countries and our cities.

Homily, 25 March 2017

———

A salad with oil . . .

Jesus had finished talking about the danger of wealth, about how difficult it was for a rich man to enter the kingdom of heaven. And Peter asks him this question: 'We have abandoned everything and followed you. What will be our reward?' Jesus is generous and starts to tell Peter: 'Truly I tell you: there is no one who has left their house or brothers or sisters or mothers or fathers or fields for me and for the Gospel who has not already received in that time a hundred times as much, and brothers and sisters and mothers and children and fields . . .'

Perhaps Peter thought: 'This is a good commercial activity, following Jesus makes us earn so much, a hundred times as much.' But Jesus adds three little words: 'along with persecution'. And then you will have eternal life. Yes, you have left everything and you will receive many things here, but along with persecution.

It's like a salad with the oil of persecution. This is the reward of the Christian, and this is the way of those who want to follow Jesus. Because it is the way that he travelled himself: he was persecuted.

Homily at Domus Sanctae Marthae, 9 June 2014

———

Open your heart to the slowness of the kingdom

In the parable, Jesus teaches us that the kingdom comes into the world in a humble way and develops constantly and silently wherever it is received by hearts open to its message of hope and salvation. The Gospel teaches us that the Spirit of Jesus can bring new life to the heart of every man and can transform every situation, even those situations that seem to be hopeless. Jesus can transform, he can transform every situation! This is the message that you are called to share with your fellows: in school, in the world of work, in your families, at university and in your community. By the fact that Jesus returned from the dead we know that he has 'words of eternal life' (*Jn* 6:68) and that his Word has the power to touch every heart, to conquer evil with good and change and redeem the world.

Address, 15 August 2014

How's joy going?

Saint Paul wrote: 'Rejoice . . . the Lord is near!' Well . . . today I'd like to ask a question. But everyone carries it in their heart, in their home, like a task to perform. And it answers itself. How's joy going, in your house? How's joy going in your family? Well, you give the answer.

Dear families, you know very well: the true joy tasted in the family is not something superficial, it doesn't come from things, from favourable conditions . . . True joy comes from a profound harmony between people, which everyone feels in their heart, and which makes us feel the beauty of being together, of supporting each other along the path of life. But at the root of this feeling of deep joy there is the presence of God, the presence of God in the family; there is his welcoming, merciful love that is respectful to everyone. And above all, a patient love: patience is a virtue of God and it teaches us in the family to have that patient love for one another. Having patience among ourselves. Patient love. Only God can create the harmony of differences. If God's love is lacking, the family too loses its harmony, self-centredness prevails and joy is extinguished. On the other hand, the family that experiences the joy of faith communicates it spontaneously. That family is the salt of the earth and light of the world, it is leavened for society as a whole.

Homily, 27 October 2013

Do not curb your dreams

I wish to state this clearly to the young, whose youth and openness to the future makes them open-hearted and generous. At times uncertainty, worries about the future and the problems they daily encounter can risk paralysing their youthful enthusiasm and shattering their dreams, to the point where they can think that it is not worth the effort to get involved, that the God of the Christian faith is somehow a limit on their freedom. Dear young friends, never be afraid to go out from yourselves and begin the journey! The Gospel is the message which brings freedom to our lives; it transforms them and makes them all the more beautiful.

Message for the World Day of Vocations, 29 March 2015

———

You don't feel fulfilled?
Abandon yourself to the arms of God

So often we are unable to grasp God's design, and we realize that we are incapable of assuring ourselves of happiness and eternal life. It is precisely in the experience of our limitations and our poverty, however, that the Spirit comforts us and allows us to see that the only important thing is to allow ourselves to be led to Jesus in the arms of his Father.

General audience, 11 June 2014

The path of life of the saints (and yours)

If there is one thing that characterizes the saints it is that they are truly *happy*. They have discovered the secret of authentic happiness, which dwells in the depths of the soul and whose source lies in the love of God. That is why the saints are called blessed.

Homily, 1 November 2016

———

God consoles you like a mother

Just as a mother takes on the burdens and trials of her children, so God loves to shoulder our sins and our worries. He, who knows us and loves us infinitely, is receptive to our prayers and can dry our tears. Every time he looks at us he is moved and touched, with a visceral love, because apart from the evil of which we are capable, we are still his children; he wants to take us in his arms, protect us, free us from dangers and from evil. Let these words that he addresses to us echo in our hearts: 'Like a mother, I will comfort you.'

Homily, 1 October 2016

———

The image of Christ and your fulfilment

Those who believe come to see themselves in the light of the faith which they profess: Christ is the mirror in which they find their own image fully realized. And just as Christ gathers to himself all those who believe and makes them his body, so the Christian comes to see himself as a member of this body, in an essential relationship with all other believers.

Lumen fidei, 22

———

Be a child in the embrace of the Spirit

When the Holy Spirit takes up residence in our hearts, he instils within it consolation and peace, and leads us to feel as we are: small, with that attitude, so often recommended by Jesus in the Gospel, of those who place all their worries and expectations in God, and who feel enveloped and sustained by his warmth and his protection, just like a child with his father! This is what the Holy Spirit does in our hearts: he makes us feel like children in our father's arms. In this sense, then, we can clearly understand how the fear of God can assume within us the form of docility, of gratitude and praise, filling our hearts with hope.

General audience, 11 June 2014

———

I want a love that lasts for ever

The heart of the human being aspires to great things, to important values, to deep friendships, to bonds that strengthen rather than break in the trials of life. The human being aspires to love and to be loved. This is our deepest aspiration: to love and be loved; that much is certain. The culture of provisionality does not increase our liberty, but deprives us of our true destiny, of truer and more authentic goals. It is a life in pieces. It is sad to reach a certain age, look at the path that we have taken and find that it has been made of different pieces, without unity, without finality: entirely provisional . . .

Address, 5 July 2014

————

In an orphaned age, you have a Father

God is not a remote and anonymous being: he is our refuge, the source of our serenity and our peace. He is the rock of our salvation, to which we can cling in the certainty that we will not fall; he who clings to God never falls! He is our defence against the evil that always lies in waiting. God for us is the great friend, the ally, the Father, but we do not always realize. We do not realize that we have a friend, an ally, a Father who loves us, and prefer to rely on immediate goods that we can touch, contingent goods, forgetting, and sometimes refusing, the supreme good, God's paternal love. Feeling that he is the Father, in this orphaned age, is so important! Orphan in this world, feeling that he is the Father.

Angelus, 26 February 2017

I can't cope . . .

We can't cope on our own. Faced with the pressure of events and fashions, we will never be able to find the right path on our own, and even if we did find it, we wouldn't have enough strength to persevere, to confront the unforeseen climbs and obstacles. And it is here that the Lord Jesus' invitation comes in: 'If you want to . . . follow me'. He invites us to go with him on our journey, not to exploit us, not to make us slaves, but to make us free. Within this freedom he invites us to go with him on our journey. That is how it is. Only *together with* Jesus, praying to him and following him, do we find the clarity of vision and the strength to carry him onwards. He loves us definitively, he has chosen us definitively, he has given himself definitively to each of us. He is our defender and our big brother, and he will be our only judge. How beautiful it is to be able to confront the changeable events of life in the company of Jesus, to have with us his Person and his message! He does not take away our autonomy or our freedom; on the contrary, strengthening our frailty, he allows us to be truly free, free to do good, strong to go on doing it, capable of forgiving and capable of asking for forgiveness. This is Jesus coming with us, this is what the Lord is like!

Address, 5 July 2014

Do not withdraw, do not allow yourself to be asphyxiated, do not stay a prisoner

Do not withdraw into yourselves, do not allow yourselves to be asphyxiated by little domestic disputes, do not remain prisoners of your problems. These will be resolved if you go out and help others to solve their problems and announce the good news. You will find life by giving life, hope by giving hope, love by loving.

Letter to all consecrated people, 21 November 2014

———

Come out of yourself: you will receive a hundred times as much

At the root of all Christian vocation there is this fundamental movement of the experience of faith: believing means leaving oneself, leaving the comfort and rigidity of our own self to centre our life in Jesus Christ: to abandon, like Abraham, our own land, setting out confidently, in the knowledge that God will point out the way towards the new land. This 'coming out' should not be understood as contempt for our own life, our own feeling, our own humanity; on the contrary, those who set off following Christ find life in abundance, making themselves wholly available to God and his kingdom. Jesus says: 'Truly I tell you, no one who has left home or brothers or sisters or mother or father or children or fields for me will fail to receive a hundred times as much in this present age, and in the age to come eternal life' (Mt 19:29). All of this is deeply rooted in love.

Message for the World Day of Vocations, 29 March 2015

Break down the barriers of fear

It was the first word that the archangel Gabriel addressed to the Virgin: 'Rejoice, Mary, full of grace, the Lord is with you' (*Lk* 1:28). The lives of those who have discovered Jesus are filled with inner joy so great that nothing and no one can take it away from them. Christ gives his people the strength required not to be unhappy or disheartened, thinking that problems have no solutions. Supported by this truth, the Christian does not doubt that what is done with love produces a serene joy, the sister of the hope that breaks down the barrier of fear and opens the door to a promising future.

Message, 8 September 2014

Don't settle for a 'miniature' life

Do you really aspire to happiness? In a time when we are attracted by so many semblances of happiness, you risk settling for little, having a 'miniature' idea of life. Aspire to great things! Enlarge your hearts! As the blessed Pier Giorgio Frassati said, 'living without a faith, without a patrimony to defend, without supporting the truth in a continuous struggle, is not living but getting by. We must never get by, we must live' (Letter to I. Bonini, 28 February 1925).

Message for World Youth Day, 21 January 2014

Let the Spirit open your heart

This is why we have such need of this gift of the Holy Spirit. The fear of God makes us aware that everything comes from grace, and that our true strength lies entirely in following the Lord Jesus and letting the Father pour down upon us his goodness and his mercy. Open your hearts, so that the goodness and mercy of God may come to us. This is what the Holy Spirit does with the gift of the fear of God: it opens hearts. An open heart so that forgiveness, mercy, goodness, the caresses of the Father may come to us, because we are infinitely beloved children.

General audience, 11 June 2014

It takes courage today

Today is a time of mission and a time of courage! Courage to strengthen unsteady steps, to reacquire the taste of committing oneself to the Gospel, to regain trust in the strength that mission brings. It is a time for courage, even though having courage does not mean having a guarantee of success. Courage is required of us to fight, not necessarily to win, to proclaim, not necessarily to convert. Courage is required of us to be alternative in the world, but without becoming polemical or aggressive. Courage is required of us to open ourselves to everything, without ever reducing the absoluteness and uniqueness of Christ, the sole saviour of all.

Courage is required of us to resist disbelief, without being arrogant. We also have to have the courage of the tax collector in today's Gospel, who in his humility did not even dare raise his eyes to heaven, but beat his breast, saying, 'Oh God, have mercy on me, a sinner.' Today is a time for courage! Today courage is needed!

Angelus, 23 October 2016

———

God in the heart

The consolation we need, amid the turbulent events of life, is the presence of God in our hearts. Because his presence in us is the source of true consolation that remains, that frees us from evil, brings peace and makes joy grow.

Homily, 1 October 2016

———

Who annoys Pope Francis?

When I hear a young boy or girl talking about the Lord, or a catechist, I don't know, anybody, I get annoyed. We talk about the Lord with a certain sadness. He said *joy*: that is the secret. Talking about the Lord *with joy*, that is what we call *Christian witness*. You understand?

Meeting, 15 January 2017

———

Be a person who sings life

Be people who sing life, who sing faith. This is important: don't just recite the *Credo*, recite faith, know faith, but sing faith! That's it. Tell faith, live faith with joy, and this is called 'singing faith'. And it's not me saying it! Saint Augustine said it 1,600 years ago: 'sing faith'!

Address, 3 May 2014

————

The still of fear

It's easier to believe in a fantasy that I live in Christ! It is easier to go to a fortune teller who predicts your future, who reads the cards for you, than to have faith in a victorious Christ, a Christ who has defeated death! An idea, a figment of the imagination, is easier than docility to this Lord who returns from death and you know what he is inviting you to do! This process of relativizing faith to such an extent in the end brings us far from the encounter, brings us far from God's caress. It is as if we 'distilled' the reality of the encounter with Jesus Christ in the still of fear, in the still of excessive certainty, wanting to control the encounter ourselves. The disciples were afraid of joy . . . and so are we.

Homily, 24 April 2014

Happiness can't be bought

Happiness can't be bought. And when you buy a happiness, you realize that the happiness has gone . . . The happiness that is bought does not last. Only the happiness of love is the one that lasts.

And the path of love is simple: love God and love your neighbour, your brother, the one who is close to you, the one who needs love and needs so many things. 'But, Father, how do I know if I love God?' Simply, if you love your neighbour, if you don't hate, if you don't have hatred in your heart, you love God. That is the certain proof.

Address, 15 August 2014

———

Do you also want to go away?

Jesus calls to us . . . to answer to his proposal of life, to decide which path we want to take to reach true joy. This is a great challenge to faith. Jesus was not afraid to ask his disciples if they really wanted to follow him or if they wanted to go away (cf. *Jn* 6:670). And Simon, called Peter, had the courage to answer: 'Lord, where will we go? You have words of eternal life' (*Jn* 6:68). If you also want to say 'yes' to Jesus, your life will be filled with meaning, so it will be fertile.

Message for World Youth Day, 21 January 2014

Look at your talents, look at your limits: you aren't alone!

People who are capable of recognizing their own talents and their own limits, who know how to see in their own days, even the days most plunged in darkness, the signs of the presence of the Lord. To rejoice because the Lord has called you to share responsibility of the mission in his Church. To rejoice because you are not alone on this path: the Lord goes with you, your bishops and priests are there to support you, your parish communities, your diocesan communities with whom you share your path. You are not alone!

Address, 3 May 2014

———

Confront life as one who is strong, not sated

It is very sad to see young people who are 'sated' but weak. Writing to the young, Saint John said: 'You are strong and the Word of God lives in you and you have conquered the Evil one.' Young people who choose Christ are strong, they are nourished by his Word and they do not 'gorge themselves' on other things! Have the courage to go against the current. Have the courage of true happiness! Say no to the culture of provisionality, of superficiality and discards, which does not support you enough to assume responsibility and confront the big challenges of life!

Message for World Youth Day, 21 January 2014

Never fear risking gaiety

In the passage from the Gospel that we have just heard the disciples cannot believe the joy that they have, because they cannot believe because of that joy. So says the Gospel. Let us look at the scene: Jesus is risen, the disciples of Emmaus have related their experience, Peter too tells that he has seen him. Then the Lord himself appears in the room and says to them: 'Peace be upon you.' Various emotions fill the hearts of the disciples: fear, surprise, doubt and, finally, joy. Joy so great that because of that joy 'they could not believe'. They were astonished, shocked, and Jesus, almost with a hint of a smile, asks them for something eat and begins to explain the Scriptures, opening their minds so that they can understand them. It is the moment of wonder, of the encounter with Jesus Christ, where so much joy does not seem real to us; even more, assuming joy and gaiety at that moment seems risky to us, and we feel tempted to take refuge in scepticism, in 'not exaggerating'.

Homily, 24 April 2014

———

The style of Jesus is our freedom

By making himself poor, Jesus did not seek poverty for its own sake but, as Saint Paul says, *'that by his poverty you might become rich'*. This is not a mere play on words or a catch phrase. Rather it sums up God's logic, the logic of love, the logic of the Incarnation and the cross. God did not rain his salvation down on us from above, like someone giving alms from their abundance out of a sense of altruism and piety. Christ's love is not like that! When Jesus went down into the waters of the Jordan and was baptised by John the Baptist, he did not do so because he was in need of repentance, of conversion; he did it to put himself among the people, who needed forgiveness, among us sinners, and to take on the weight of our sins. This is the life that he chose, to console us, to free us from our misery.

Message for Lent, 2014

———

Everyone, let us say it:
With Jesus joy finds its home!

Jesus has come to bring joy to everyone and forever. This is not a joy that is merely hoped for or postponed to paradise: here on earth we are sad but in paradise we will be joyful. No! It is not that, but a joy that is already real and can be experienced now, because *Jesus himself is our joy*, and with Jesus joy finds its home, as your sign there says: with Jesus joy finds its home. Everyone, let us say it: 'With Jesus joy finds its home.' And is there joy without Jesus? No! Well done! He is living, he is the Risen One, and he works in us and among us, particularly with the Word and the Sacraments.

Angelus, 14 December 2014

Come to me, all you who are weary!

There is a saying of Jesus, in the Gospel of Matthew, which speaks to us: 'Come to me, all you who are weary and burdened, and I will give you rest' (*Mt* 11:28). Life is often a struggle, and many times it is also tragic . . .! Work is tiring, looking for work is tiring. And finding work today requires such an effort! But that is not what is most burdensome in life: what weighs more heavily than all of these things is the lack of love. It is burdensome not to receive a smile, not to be welcomed. Certain silences are burdensome, sometimes even in the family, between husband and wife, between parents and children, among brothers and sisters. Without love the burden is made even heavier, unbearable. I am thinking of old people on their own, of families who struggle because they receive no help to support those at home who need special attention and treatment. 'Come to me, all you who are weary and oppressed,' Jesus says.

Address, 26 October 2013

———

Source, manifestation, soul

The Father is the source of joy. The Son is its manifestation, and the Holy Spirit its provider. Immediately after praising the Father, as the evangelist Matthew says, Jesus invites us: 'Come to me, all you who are weary and oppressed, and I will give you rest. Take my yoke upon you and learn from me, for

I am gentle and humble in heart, and you will find rest for your souls. For my yoke is easy and my burden is light' (11:28–30). 'The joy of the Gospel fills the hearts and the whole lives of those who encounter Jesus. Those who allow themselves to be saved by him are freed from sin, from sadness, from inner emptiness, from isolation. With Jesus Christ joy is always born and reborn' (*Evangelii gaudium*, 1). The Virgin Mary had a thoroughly unique experience of such an encounter with Jesus, and became '*causa nostrae laetitiae*'. The disciples, however, received the calling to be with Jesus and be sent by him to evangelize, so they were filled with joy. Why do we too not step into that river of joy?

Message, 8 June 2014

———

Leave behind your water jar

In the Gospel story of the Samaritan woman we find the instruction to 'leave behind our water jar', the symbol of all that is apparently important, but that loses value in the face of the 'love of God'. We all have one, or more than one! I ask you, and I ask myself: 'What is your inner water jar, the one that weighs upon you, that takes you far from God?' Let us leave it aside for a while, and with our hearts hear the voice of Jesus offering us a different water, a different water that brings us close to the Lord. We are called to rediscover the importance and the meaning of our Christian life, which begins with Baptism and, like the Samaritan woman, to bear witness to our brothers and sisters. Joy! Bear witness to the joy of our encounter with Jesus, because I have said that every encounter with Jesus changes our lives, and every encounter with Jesus fills us with joy, the joy that comes from within. That is what the Lord is like. And tell people how many wonderful things the Lord can do in our hearts, when we have the courage to leave our water jar behind.

Angelus, 13 March 2014

Go out of yourself and seek the light

He who wants the light goes out of himself and searches: he does not remain withdrawn, motionless, looking at what is going on around him, but puts his own life on the line; he goes out of himself. The Christian life is a *constant journey*, made of hope, made of seeking; a journey that, like that of the Magi, goes on even when the star momentarily disappears from sight. On this journey there are also pitfalls that must be avoided: superficial and worldly chatter, which hinders our steps; the paralysing whims of egoism; the potholes of pessimism, which trip up hope.

Angelus, 6 January 2017

Do not settle for small goals

Do not let yourselves be robbed of the desire to build big and solid things in your life! This is what takes you forward. Do not settle for small goals! Aspire to happiness, have the courage for it, the courage to go out of yourselves, fully to play out your future with Jesus.

Address, 5 July 2014

————

Reject 'low price' offers

If you really bring the deepest aspirations out of your hearts, you will realize that there is within you an inextinguishable desire for happiness, and that will allow you to unmask and reject the many 'low price' offers you find around you. When we seek success, pleasure, possession in an egoistic way and make idols of them, we can also feel moments of intoxication, a false sense of satisfaction; but in the end we become slaves, we are never satisfied, we are driven to keep on seeking more.

Message for the Day of Mercy, 21 January 2014

————

The joy of God is the presence of Jesus among us

On the third Sunday of advent the liturgy proposes a different inner attitude with which to experience waiting for the

Lord, which is joy. The joy of Jesus, as that sign there says: 'With Jesus joy finds its home'. There, the joy of Jesus suggests to us!

Man's heart desires joy. We all desire joy, every family, every people aspires to happiness. But what is the joy that that Christian is called to experience and bear witness to? It is the one that comes from the *nearness of God*, from his *presence* in our lives. Since Jesus entered the story with his birth in Bethlehem, mankind has received the germ of the kingdom of God, like a patch of ground receiving the seed, the promise of a future harvest. You don't need to look anywhere else!

Angelus, 14 December 2014

———

Love beauty, seek truth

For me, a young person who loves truth and seeks it, loves goodness and is good, is a good person, and seeks and loves beauty, is on a good path and is bound to find God! Sooner or later he will find it! But the road is long and some people don't find it in life. They don't find it in a conscious way. But they are so true and honest with themselves, so good and such lovers of beauty that in the end they have very mature personalities, capable of encountering God, which is always a grace. Because encountering God is a grace.

We can take that journey . . . Some meet him in other people . . . It is a journey to travel . . . Each individual must encounter him personally. God is not encountered by hear-say, and you can't pay to meet him. It is a personal journey, we have to meet him like that. I don't know if I've answered your question . . .

Meeting with young people, 31 March 2014

————

A scene filled with light

Jesus rode into Jerusalem. The crowd of disciples accompanied him, celebrating, cloaks were laid out in front of him, there was talk of the miracles that he had performed, a cry of praise rose up: 'Blessed the king who comes in the name of the Lord. Peace in heaven and glory in the highest' (*Lk* 19:38).

Crowd, celebration, blessing, peace: it is a climate of joy that they are breathing. Jesus has revealed much hope, above all to the hearts of the humble, simple, poor, forgotten people, the ones who don't count in the eyes of the world. He understood human miseries, he showed the face of God's mercy and he bent down to cure the body and the soul.

Homily, 24 March 2013

————

When the almond tree flowers

The good always attracts us, truth attracts us, life, happiness, beauty attract us . . . Jesus is the meeting point of this mutual attraction, this double movement. He is God and man: Jesus.

God and man. But who took the initiative? God, always! God's love always comes before our own! He always takes the initiative. He waits for us, he invites us, the initiative is always his. Jesus is God made man, made flesh, he is born for us. The new star that appears to the Magi was a sign of the birth of Christ. Had they not seen the star, these men would not have set out. The light goes before us, truth goes before us, beauty precedes us. God goes before us. The Prophet Isaiah said that God is like the flower of the almond tree. Why? Because in that region the almond is the first to flower. And God always goes ahead, he is always the first to seek us, he takes the first step.

Angelus, 6 January 2014

———

Saint Teresa of Avila, the mistress of happiness

Teresa of Jesus asks her sisters to 'go cheerfully about whatever services you are ordered to do' (*The Way of Perfection* 18, 5). True holiness is a joy, because 'an unhappy saint is a pitiful saint'. Saints, before being courageous heroes, are the fruit of God's grace to mankind. Every saint shows us a feature of the multifaceted face of God. In Saint Teresa we contemplate the God who, being 'sovereign Majesty, eternal wisdom' (*Poems* 2), reveals himself to be close by and a companion who delights in conversing with men: God rejoices with us. And feeling his love, an infectious joy that she was unable to hide was born in the Saint, which she transmitted to her surroundings. That joy is a journey which must be followed throughout life. It is not instantaneous, superficial, tumultuous. It must be sought 'at the beginning' (*Life* 13, 1). It expresses the inner joy of the soul, it is humble and 'modest' (cf. *The Book of Foundations* 12, 1). It is not reached by an easy path that bypasses sacrifice, suffering or the cross, but is found by enduring labour and pain (cf. *Life* 6, 2; 30, 8), looking to the crucifix and seeking the Risen One (cf. *The Way of Perfection* 26, 4). So Saint Teresa's joy was neither selfish nor self-referential, but like that of heaven, it consists in 'joy in the rejoicings of all' (*The Way of Perfection* 30, 5), placing oneself at the service of others with unselfish love. As she told one of her monasteries in difficulty, the Saint would also tell us today, especially the young: 'Do not stop going cheerfully about!' (*Letter* 284, 4). The Gospel is not a bag of lead that one drags arduously, but a font of joy that fills the heart with God and impels it to serve one's brothers!

Message, 15 October 2014

What will my path be?

I too asked this question in my day: which path must I choose? But you don't need to choose a path: the Lord must choose it! Jesus has chosen it, you must hear him and ask: 'Lord, what must I do?' This is the prayer that a young person must make: 'Lord, what do you want of me?' And with the prayer and advice of some true friends – laymen, priests, nuns, bishops,

Popes . . . the Pope too can give good advice – with the advice of these, find the path that the Lord wants for you.

Address, 15 August 2014

———

Praise of rest

Rest is necessary for the salvation of our minds and our bodies, and yet it is often so difficult to achieve, because of the many demands that weigh upon us. Rest is also essential for our spiritual health, so that we may listen to the voice of God and understand what he asks of us.

Address, 16 January 2015

———

Cultivate trust, in people and in God

So many times we trust a doctor: it is good, because the doctor is there to heal us; we trust a person: brothers and sisters can help us. It is good to have this human trust between us. But we forget trust in the Lord: this is the key to success in life. Trust in the Lord, let us trust the Lord! 'Lord, look at my life: I am in darkness, I have this difficulty, I have this sin . . .' all that we have: 'Look at this: I am trusting in you!' And this is a wager that we must make: trusting in him, and never be disappointed. Never, never! Feel good, boys and girls who are starting your lives now: Jesus never disappoints. Never. This is the witness of John: Jesus, the good, the meek, who will end up as a lamb, killed. Without crying out. He came to save us, to take away our sin. Mine, yours, and the sin of the world: everything, everything.

Homily, 19 January 2014

———

Pray and give thanks . . .

The apostle Paul says to the Thessalonians: 'Brothers, always rejoice'. And how can I rejoice? He says: 'Pray, without interruption, give thanks in everything.' We find Christian joy in prayer, it comes from prayer, and also from giving thanks to God: 'Thank you, Lord, for so many beautiful things!'

Homily, 14 December 2014

———

Prepare a house for Jesus in your heart

Joseph was chosen by God to be the putative father of Jesus and husband of Mary. As Christians, you too feel called, like Joseph, to prepare a house for Jesus. Prepare a house for Jesus! You prepare a house for him in your hearts, in your families, in your parishes and your communities.

Address, 16 January 2015

Think about good things

Give thanks. And how do I give thanks? Remember your life, and think about so many things that life has given you, 'But, Father, it is true, but I have received so many bad things!' 'Yes, it's true, it happens to everyone. But think about the good things.' 'I had a Christian family, Christian parents, thank God I have a job, my family doesn't suffer from hunger, we are all healthy . . .' I don't know, so many things, and give thanks to the Lord for it. And this accustoms us to joy. Pray, give thanks . . .

Homily, 14 December 2014

THE SECRET OF LIFE

'The Beatitudes are the path, the goal towards the homeland.
They are the path of life that the Lord points out to us
so that we may follow in his footsteps.'
1 November 2016

———

God goes on seeking

As he did yesterday, God goes on seeking his allies, he goes on seeking men and women who are capable of believing, capable of recording events, feeling part of his people to cooperate with the creativity of the Spirit. God continues to walk our neighbourhoods and streets, going everywhere in search of hearts capable of listening to his invitation and make it flesh here and now. To paraphrase Saint Ambrose in his comment on this passage, we may say: God goes on seeking hearts like Mary's, willing to believe even in quite extraordinary conditions.

Homily, 25 March 2017

We are not made for small matters

We trust in God's action! With him we can do great things; he will make us feel the joy of being his disciples, his witnesses. Bet on great ideals, on big things. We Christians are not chosen by the Lord for small matters, always go beyond, towards the big things. Play life for big ideals, young people!

Homily, 28 April 2013

Don't you feel how worried your heart is?

The quest for happiness is common to all people of all times and all ages. God has put in the heart of every man and every woman an irrepressible desire for happiness, for fulfilment. Do you not notice that your hearts are worried and in constant search of a good that can satisfy their thirst for the infinite?

Message for World Youth Day, 31 January 2015

You will experience peace

In proclaiming the Beatitudes, Jesus invites us to follow him, to walk with him the way of love, the only one that leads to eternal life. It is not an easy path, but the Lord assures us of his grace and never leaves us on our own. Poverty, afflictions, humiliations, a struggle for justice, the efforts of daily conversion, the fight to experience the call to holiness, per-secutions and many other challenges are present in our lives. But if we open the door to Jesus, if we let him into our story, if we share with him our joys and griefs, we will experience a peace and a joy that only God, infinite love, can give.

Message for World Youth Day, 21 January 2014

———

The way of true fulfilment

It always does us a lot of good to read and meditate upon the Beatitudes! Jesus proclaimed them in his first great sermon, on the shore of Lake Galilee. There was a huge crowd and he climbed on to the hill to teach his disciples, which was why that sermon is called 'the sermon on the mount'. In the Bible, the mountain is seen as a place where God is revealed, and Jesus preaching on the hill presents himself to us as a divine teacher, a new Moses. And what does he communicate to us? Jesus communicates the way of life, the way that he walks himself, or in fact, that he himself *is*, and he proposes it as the *way of true happiness*.

Message for World Youth Day, 21 January 2014

———

Never let yourself be blinded by presumption

God has hidden all of this from those who are too full of themselves and claim to know everything already. It is as if they are blinded by their own presumption and leave no room for God. We might easily think of some of Jesus' contemporaries whom he admonished on several occasions, but it is a danger that has always existed, and that concerns each of us. In fact, the 'little' people are the humble, the simple, the poor, the marginalized, the ones without a voice, the weary and the oppressed, whom Jesus called 'blessed'. We might easily think of Mary, of Joseph, of the fishermen of Galilee, and the disciples called along the way, in the course of his sermon.

Message, 8 June 2014

———

The whole kingdom of God is in the Beatitudes

Throughout his life, from his birth in the stable in Bethlehem to his death on the cross and the resurrection, Jesus embodied the Beatitudes. All the promises of the kingdom of God are fulfilled in him.

Message for World Youth Day, 21 January 2014

———

You are blessed only when you are converted

Jesus manifests God's will to lead mankind to happiness. This message was already present in the words of the prophets: God is close to the poor and the oppressed and frees them from those who mistreat them. But in this sermon

Jesus follows a particular path. He begins with the word *blessed*, that is, *happy*; he goes on to indicate the *condition* of being so; and he concludes with a *promise*. The cause of blessedness, that is, of happiness, lies not in the requisite condition – for example 'poor in spirit', 'mourning', 'hungry for righteousness', 'persecuted' – but in the subsequent promise, to be welcomed with faith as a gift of God. One starts from a condition of hardship in order to open oneself to God's gift and enter the new world, the 'kingdom' proclaimed by Jesus. This is not an automatic mechanism, but a way of life in following the Lord, through which the reality of hardship and affliction is seen from a new perspective and experienced according to the conversion that comes about. One is not *blessed* if one is not *converted*, capable of appreciating and experiencing the gifts of God.

Angelus, 29 January 2017

―――

The quest for happiness

The word *blessed*, or *happy*, appears nine times in the sermon on the mount, which is Jesus' first great sermon (cf. *Mt* 5:1–12). It is like a refrain that reminds us of the calling of the Lord to walk with him along a path which, in spite of all challenges, is the way of true happiness.

Message for World Youth Day, 31 January 2015

The Magnificat of Mary introduces the Beatitudes to us

The *Magnificat* thus introduces us to the Beatitudes, the primordial summary and law of the Gospel message. In the light of it, today, we feel driven to ask for a grace, that very Christian grace that the future . . . may be forged by the poor and by those who suffer, by the humble, by those who hunger and thirst for justice, by the merciful, by the pure in heart, by the peacemakers, by those who are persecuted for the sake of Christ's name, 'for theirs is the kingdom of heaven' (cf. *Mt* 5:1–11). May the grace be forged by those who today are relegated to the category of slaves, of objects to be exploited or simply rejected, by the idolatrous system of the throwaway culture.

Homily, 12 December 2014

———

Those who trust in the Lord

The first Beatitude . . . declares that the *poor in spirit* are happy because the kingdom of heaven belongs to them. In a time when many people are suffering because of the financial crisis, it might seem strange to link poverty and happiness. How can we see poverty as a blessing? First of all, let us try to understand what it means to be '*poor in spirit*'. When the Son of God became man, he chose the path of poverty and self-emptying. As Saint Paul said in his letter to the Philippians: 'Let the same mind be in you that was in Christ Jesus who, though he was in the form of God, did not count equality with God a thing to be grasped, but emptied himself, taking the form of a servant, being born in human likeness' (2:5–7). Jesus is God who strips himself of his glory. Here we see God's choice to be poor: he was rich and yet he became poor in order to enrich us through his poverty (cf. 2 Cor 8:9). This is the mystery we contemplate in the crib when we see the Son of God lying in a manger and later on the cross, where his despoliation reaches its peak. The Greek adjective *ptochós* (poor) does not have a purely material meaning. It means 'a beggar', and should be seen as linked to the Jewish notion of the *anawim*, 'the poor of Yahweh', which evokes humility, the awareness of one's own limits, of one's own existential of poverty. The *anawim* trust in the Lord, they know how to rely on him.

Message for World Youth Day, 21 January 2014

———

Are you a 'the more I have, the more I want' sort of person?

'Blessed are the poor in spirit, because theirs is the kingdom of heaven' (Mt 5:4). The poor in spirit are those who have assumed the feelings and attitudes of the poor people who, in their condition, do not rebel, but who know how to be humble, meek and open to God's grace. The happiness of the poor – of the poor in spirit – has a twofold dimension: with regard to *riches* and with regard to *God*. With regard to possessions, material possessions, this poverty in spirit is sobriety: not necessarily sacrifice, but the ability to savour the essence, to share; the

ability to renew every day the wonder at the goodness of things, without being weighed down in the darkness of voracious consumption. The more I have, the more I want; the more I have, the more I want: this is voracious consumption. It kills the soul. Men or women who do this, who have this attitude, 'the more I have, the more I want', are not happy and will not attain happiness. With regard to God, it is praise and recognition that the world is a blessing and that at its origin lies the creative love of the Father. But it is also openness to him, docility to his lordship: it is he, the Lord, it is he, the Great one. I am not great because I have so many things! It is he! He who wanted the world for mankind, and wanted it so that men and women would be happy.

Angelus, 29 January 2017

———

Mary, poor in spirit

We realize how much we need to be converted, so that the logic of *being more* will prevail over that of *having more*! The saints can best help us to understand the profound meaning of the Beatitudes . . .

The *Magnificat*, the Canticle of Mary, poor in spirit, is also the song of everyone who lives by the Beatitudes. The joy of the Gospel arises from a poor heart, which, in its poverty, rejoices and marvels at the works of God, like the heart of Our Lady, whom all generations call 'blessed' (cf. *Lk* 1:48). May Mary, Mother of the poor and Star of the new evangelization, help us to live the Gospel, to embody the Beatitudes in our lives, and to have the courage always to be happy.

Message for World Youth Day, 21 January 2014

The joys of poor believers

The most beautiful and spontaneous joys that I have seen in the course of my life are those of very poor people who have little to cling to. I also remember the genuine joy of those who, even in the midst of great professional commitments, have been able to keep a believing, generous and simple heart.

Evangelii gaudium, 7

Be a beggar before God

As Saint Thérèse of the Child Jesus clearly saw, by his incarnation Jesus came among us as a poor beggar, asking for our love. The Catechism of the Catholic Church tells us that 'man is a beggar before God' and that prayer is the meeting of God's thirst and our own.

Saint Francis of Assisi perfectly understood the secret of the Beatitude of the poor in spirit. Indeed, when Jesus spoke to him through the leper and from the crucifix, Francis recognized both God's grandeur and his own lowliness. In his prayer, the Poor Man of Assisi would spend hours asking the Lord: 'Who are you?' 'Who am I?' He renounced an affluent and carefree life to marry 'Lady Poverty', to imitate Jesus and follow the Gospel to the letter. Francis lived the *imitation of Christ in his poverty and the love of the poor* – for him the two were inseparable, like two sides of a coin.

Message for World Youth Day, 21 January 2014

———

Choose richness in poverty and poverty in richness

So what is this poverty by which Christ frees us and enriches us? It is his way of loving us, his way of being our neighbour, just as the Good Samaritan was a neighbour to the man left half dead by the side of the road (cf. *Lk* 10:25ff). What gives us true freedom, true salvation and true happiness is the compassion, tenderness and solidarity of his love. Christ's poverty which enriches us is his making himself flesh, his bearing our sins and weaknesses as an expression of God's infinite mercy to us. Christ's poverty is the greatest treasure of all: Jesus' wealth is that of his boundless confidence in God the Father, his constant trust, his desire always and only to do the will of the Father and give glory to him. Jesus is rich like a child who feels loved and loves its parents and does not doubt their love and tenderness for an instant. The wealth of Jesus lies in his being *the Son*, his unique relationship with the Father is the sovereign prerogative of this Messiah who is poor. When Jesus asks us to take up his 'yoke which is easy', he invites us to enrich ourselves with his 'rich poverty' and 'poor richness', to share with him his filial and fraternal

Spirit, to become sons and daughters in the Son, brothers and sisters in the First-born Brother (cf. *Rom* 8:29).

It has been said that the only true sadness lies in not being a saint (Léon Bloy); we could also say that there is only one true misery: not living as children of God and brothers and sisters of Christ.

Message for Lent 2014

————

Do you have open hands and an open heart?

The poor in spirit is the Christian who does not rely on himself, on material wealth, is not obstinate in his own opinions, but listens with respect and willingly defers to the decisions of others. If in our communities there were more of the poor in spirit, there would be fewer divisions, disagreements and controversies! Humility, like charity, is an essential virtue for living together in Christian communities. The poor, in this evangelical sense, appear to be those who keep alive the objective of the kingdom of heaven, offering a glimpse of it revealed as a seed in the fraternal community which favours sharing over ownership. I would like to emphasize this: to favour sharing over ownership. Always having the heart and hands *open* [he gestures], not *closed* [he gestures]. When the heart is *closed* [he gestures], it is a shrunken heart. It doesn't even know how to love. When the heart is *open* [he gestures], it is on the path of love.

Angelus, 29 January 2017

The Church is the home of the afflicted

The Church, which is missionary by her nature, carries out the service of charity to all as a fundamental prerogative. Universal brotherhood and solidarity are innate to her life and to her mission in the world and for the world. Evangelization, which must reach everyone, is nevertheless called to begin with the least, with the poor, with those weighed down by the burden and strain of life. In so doing the Church prolongs the mission of Christ himself, who 'came in order that they may have life, and have it abundantly' (*Jn* 10:10). The Church is the people of the Beatitudes, the home of the poor, of the afflicted, of the excluded and persecuted, of those who hunger and thirst for righteousness. You are asked to work and strive so that the ecclesial community may be ready to receive the poor with preferential love, keeping the doors of the Church open so that all may enter and find refuge in it.

Address, 9 May 2014

———

Cultivate within yourself the gift of meekness

The gift of piety means being truly able to rejoice with those who are joyful, to weep with those who are weeping, to be close to those who are anxious, to correct those who are in error, to comfort the afflicted, to welcome and give succour to those in need. There is a very close relationship between the gift of piety and meekness. The gift of piety given to us by the Holy Spirit makes us meek, it makes us calm, patient, at peace with God, meekly at the service of others.

General audience, 4 June 2014

———

Look at the future with the eyes of faith

Let us look to the future with the eyes of faith. Our sadness is a seed that will one day bear fruit in the joy that our Lord has promised to those who trust in his words: 'Blessed are you who mourn, for you will be comforted' (cf. *Mt* 5:4). [. . .] God's *compassion*, his suffering with us, gives eternal meaning and value to our struggles. Your desire to thank him for every grace and blessing, even when you have lost so much, is not only a triumph of resilience and strength [. . .] it is also a sign of God's goodness, his closeness, his tenderness, his saving power.

Homily, 17 January 2015

———

Change the world, rediscover humility

The Beatitudes are the image of Christ, and consequently of every Christian. Here I would like to mention only one: '*Blessed are the meek*'. Jesus says of himself: 'Learn from me for I am meek and lowly in heart' (*Mt* 11:29). This is his spiritual portrait and it reveals the abundance of his love. Meekness is a way of living and acting that draws us close to Jesus and to one another. It enables us to set aside everything that divides and estranges us, and constantly to find new ways to advance along the path of unity . . . The saints bring about change through meekness of heart. With that meekness, we come to understand the grandeur of God and worship him with sincere hearts. For meekness is the attitude of those who have nothing to lose, because their only wealth is God.

Homily, 1 November 2016

The weakness of the Lamb

Jesus is called the Lamb: he is the Lamb who takes away the sin of the world. Someone might think: but how can a lamb, which is so weak, a weak little lamb, how can it take away so many sins, so much wickedness? With Love. With his meekness. Jesus never ceased being a lamb: meek, good, full of love, close to the little ones, close to the poor. He was there, among the people, healing everyone, teaching, praying. Jesus, so weak, like a lamb. However, he had the strength to take all our sins upon himself, all of them. 'But, Father, you don't know my life: I have a sin that . . . I can't even carry it with a truck . . .' Many times, when we examine our conscience, we find some sins there that are truly bad. But he carries them. He came for this: to forgive, to make peace in the world, but first in the heart. Perhaps each one of us feels troubled in his heart, perhaps he experiences darkness in his heart, perhaps he feels a little sad about a fault . . . He has come to take away all of this, he gives us peace, he forgives everything. 'Behold, the Lamb of God, who takes away sin': he takes away sin, root and all! This is the salvation Jesus brings with his love and his meekness. And hearing what John the Baptist says, who bears witness to Jesus as the Saviour, our confidence in Jesus should grow.

Homily, 19 January 2014

Gossip, the enemy of meekness

Meekness in the community is a somewhat forgotten virtue. Being gentle, making room for others. There are so many other enemies of gentleness, starting with gossip, aren't there? When people prefer to tell tales, to gossip about others, to give others a few blows. These are daily events that happen to everyone, and to me too.

They are temptations of the Evil One, who does not want the Spirit to create this gentleness in Christian communities. Let us go to the parish, and the ladies of the catechesis quarrel with the ladies of Caritas [Catholic charity] . . . These conflicts always exist, in the family, in the neighbourhood, even among friends. And this is not new life. When the Spirit comes and allows us to be born to new life, he makes us gentle and kind, not judgemental: the only judge is the Lord. [. . .] If, with the grace of the Spirit, we succeed in never gossiping, it will be a great and beautiful step forward and will do everyone good. Let us ask the Lord to show us and the world the beauty and fulfilment of this new life, of being born of the Spirit, of treating each other with kindness, with respect. Let us ask for this grace for us all.

Homily at Domus Sanctae Marthae, 9 April 2013

———

Don't be dazzled . . .

Jesus' light is a humble light. It is not a light that imposes itself, it is humble. It is a gentle light, with the strength of meekness; it is a light that speaks to the heart and it is also a light given by the cross. If we, in our inner light, are gentle people, we hear the voice of Jesus in our heart and look fearlessly at the cross in the light of Jesus . . . We must always distinguish: where Jesus is there is always humility, gentleness, love and the cross. We will never find Jesus without humility, without gentleness, without love and without the cross. He was the first to travel this path of light. We must walk fearlessly behind him, because Jesus has the strength and the authority to give us this light.

Homily at Domus Sanctae Marthae, 3 September 2013

———

. . . imitate the tranquil light of Jesus . . .

The light of Jesus is not a light of ignorance, no, no! It is a light of wisdom, of knowledge. But it is something else as well. The light that the world offers us is an artificial light. Perhaps it is strong, stronger than Jesus' light, perhaps? Strong like a firework, like a photographic flash. In fact the light of Jesus is a gentle light, it is a tranquil light, it is a light of peace. It is like the light of Christmas Eve: unpretentious. It is a light that comes from the heart.

Homily at Domus Sanctae Marthae, 3 September 2013

———

Contemplate his suffering

Only by contemplating the suffering humanity of Jesus can we become gentle, humble, tender as he was. There is no other path. We will have to make the effort to seek Jesus; to think of his passion, of how much he suffered; think of his gentle silence. This will be our endeavour; he thinks of the rest, and he will do everything that still needs to be done. But you must do this: hide your life in God with Christ.

To bear witness? Contemplate Jesus.

To forgive? Contemplate Jesus in his suffering.

Not to hate your neighbour? Contemplate Jesus in his suffering.

Not to gossip against your neighbour? Contemplate Jesus in his suffering.

There is no other way.

Homily at Domus Sanctae Marthae, 3 September 2013

You are a lamb, don't behave like a wolf

Jesus told us, 'I send you like lambs in the midst of wolves'. Be prudent, but simple. But if we allow ourselves to be overtaken by the spirit of vanity, and plan to stand up to the wolves by making ourselves into wolves, they will eat you alive. Because if you stop being a lamb, you don't have a shepherd to defend you and you will fall into the hands of these wolves. You will be able to ask, 'Father, what is the weapon with which we can defend ourselves from these seductions, from these fireworks made by the prince of this world, by his flattery?' The weapon is the same as that of Jesus: the word of God, and then humility and gentleness. We think of Jesus when they beat him: such humility, such gentleness. He could have insulted them and instead he merely asked a meek and humble question. We think of Jesus in his passion. The prophet says of him, 'like a lamb to the slaughter, he did not cry out'. The humility. Humility and gentleness: these are the weapons that the prince of the world, the spirit of the world, cannot tolerate, because his proposals are to be worldly, they are propositions of vanity, propositions of wealth. He cannot bear humility and gentleness.

Homily at Domus Sanctae Marthae, 4 May 2013

Go again, and go and go and go

We are ashamed to tell the truth: I did this, I thought this. But shame is a true Christian virtue, and also a human one.

The capacity to be ashamed: I don't know if you can say this in Italian, but in my country we call those who cannot feel shame *sinvergüenza*. This means 'someone without shame' because they do not have the capacity to be ashamed. And being ashamed is a virtue of the humble.

Humility and gentleness are like the frame of a Christian life. A Christian always proceeds like this, in humility and gentleness. And Jesus waits for us to forgive us. We can ask him a question: then is going to Confession not going to a torture session? No! And go and praise God, because I, a sinner, have been saved by him. And is he waiting to beat me? No, to punish me with tenderness. And if I do the same thing tomorrow? Go again, and go and go and go. He always waits for us. This tenderness of the Lord, this humility, this gentleness.

Homily at Domus Sanctae Marthae, 29 April 2013

They will think you're stupid

Jesus said: no wars, no hatred! Peace, gentleness! Someone might object: 'If I am as gentle as that in life, they will think I'm an idiot'. Perhaps. However, we should let other people think this: you are meek, because with this meekness you will inherit the earth!

Homily at Domus Sanctae Marthae, 9 June 2014

Do not confuse nothing with everything

The Christian is meek, the Christian is magnanimous. He opens up his heart. And when we find Christians with their hearts shrunk, it means that they are living an egoism masked as Christianity.

Jesus had advised us: 'First seek the kingdom of God and his justice and the rest will come by itself'. The kingdom of God is everything; the rest is secondary, it is not the main thing.

All the errors of the Church, all our errors are born here: when we say to nothing that it is everything; and to everything that it doesn't matter.

Homily at Domus Sanctae Marthae, 17 June 2013

Fight for righteousness and against injustice

Blessed are those who hunger and thirst for righteousness is an affirmation addressed to those who fight for righteousness, so that there is righteousness in the world. And Jesus says: blessed are those who fight against injustice. We can see that this is a doctrine that runs counter to what the world tells us.

Homily at Domus Sanctae Marthae, 9 June 2014

Hunger for justice and thirst for dignity

Dear friends, it is certainly necessary to give bread to the hungry – this is an act of justice. But there is also a deeper hunger, the hunger for a happiness that only God can satisfy, the hunger for dignity. There is neither real promotion of the common good nor real human development when there is ignorance of the fundamental pillars that govern a nation, its non-material goods: *life*, which is a gift of God, a value always to be protected and promoted; the *family*, the foundation of coexistence and a remedy against social fragmentation; *integral education*, which cannot be reduced to the mere transmission of information for purposes of generating profit; *health*, which must seek the integral wellbeing of the person, including the spiritual dimension, essential for human balance and healthy coexistence; *security*, in the conviction that violence can be overcome only by changing human hearts.

Address, 25 July 2013

Be merciful, because you too are forgiven

Blessed are the merciful, because they will find mercy. They are the ones who forgive, they understand other people's mistakes. Jesus does not say: blessed are those who are vengeful, who avenge themselves, who say an eye for an eye, a tooth for a tooth; the ones he calls blessed are the ones who forgive, the merciful ones. And all of us are an army of the forgiven! All of us have been forgiven! And so blessed is he who walks the road of forgiveness.

Homily at Domus Sanctae Marthae, 9 June 2014

God is joyful because he is merciful!

Chapter 15 of the Gospel of Luke contains three parables of mercy: the lost sheep, the lost coin, and then the longest of them, characteristic of Saint Luke, the parable of the father of two sons, the 'prodigal' son and the son who believes he is 'righteous', who believes he is saintly. All three of these parables speak of the joy of God. God is joyful. This is interesting: God is joyful! And what is the joy of God? The joy of God is forgiving, the joy of God is forgiving! The joy of a shepherd who finds his little lamb; the joy of a woman who finds her coin; it is the joy of a father welcoming home the son who was lost, who was as though dead and has come back to life, who has come home. Here is the entire Gospel! Here! The whole Gospel, all of Christianity, is here! But make sure that it is not sentiment, it is not being a 'do-gooder'! On the contrary, mercy is the true force that can save man and the world from the 'cancer' that is sin, moral evil, spiritual evil. Only love fills the void, the negative chasms that evil opens in hearts and in history. Only love can do this, and this is God's joy!

Angelus, 15 September 2013

A *pure heart is a heart that is capable of love*

'Blessed are the pure in heart' is a phrase of Jesus' that refers to those who have a simple, pure and unsullied heart: a heart that can love with that very beautiful purity.

Homily at Domus Sanctae Marthae, 9 June 2014

The *'heart' is your capacity for love*

First of all, we need to appreciate the biblical meaning of the word *heart*. In Hebrew thought, the heart is the centre of the emotions, thoughts and intentions of the human person. Since the Bible teaches us that God does not look to appearances, but to the heart (cf. *1 Sam* 16:7), we can also say that it is from the heart that we see God. This is because the heart is really the human being in his or her totality as a unity of body and soul, in his or her ability to love and to be loved.

Message for World Youth Day, 31 January 2015

Don't *lose the clarity of existence*

As for the definition of the word *pure*, the Greek word used by the evangelist Matthew is *katharos*, which basically means *clean, pure, undefiled*. In the Gospel we see Jesus reject a certain conception of ritual purity bound to exterior practices, one which forbade all contact with things and people (including lepers and strangers) considered impure. To the Pharisees who, like so many Jews of their time, ate nothing without first performing ritual ablutions and observing the many traditions associated with cleansing vessels, Jesus responds categorically: 'There is nothing outside a man which by going into him can defile him; but the things which come out of a man are what defile him. For from within, out of the heart of man, come evil thoughts, fornication, theft, murder, adultery, coveting, wickedness, deceit, licentiousness, envy, slander, pride, foolishness' (*Mk* 7:15, 21–22).

Message for World Youth Day, 31 January 2015

Develop a human ecology

Each one of us must learn to discern what can 'defile' his or her heart and to form his or her conscience rightly and sensibly, so as to be capable of 'discerning the will of God, what is good and acceptable and perfect' (*Rom* 12:2). We need to show a healthy concern for creation, for the purity of our air, water and food, but how much more do we need to protect the purity of what is most precious of all: *our heart and our relationships*. This 'human ecology' will help us to breathe the pure air that comes from beauty, from true love, and from holiness.

Message for World Youth Day, 31 January 2015

Peace has no misunderstandings or subterfuges

'Blessed are the peacemakers'. It is so common to be a war-maker or at least a maker of misunderstandings, when I hear one of these things I go to him and I say it; and I also make a second, slightly longer version, and I deliver that. It is the world of gossip, of gossiping people, that does not make peace. And it is certainly not blessed.

Homily at Domus Sanctae Marthae, 9 June 2014

————

There is no future without peace

Peace is not simply the absence of war, but a general condition in which the human person is in harmony with him/herself, in harmony with nature and in harmony with others. This is peace. Nevertheless, silencing weapons and extinguishing the hotbeds of war is an inevitable condition to begin a journey that leads to peace in its various aspects. I think of the wars that still cause bloodshed in too many regions of the planet, of the tensions in families and in communities – but in many families, in many communities, in parishes too, there is war! – as well as heated disputes in our cities and towns between groups of different ethnic, cultural and religious extraction. We must convince ourselves, despite every appearance to the contrary, that harmony is always possible, on every level and in every situation. There is no future without proposals and plans for peace! There is no future without peace!

Angelus, 4 January 2015

———

Fight for justice, in spite of persecution!

'Blessed are those who are persecuted for justice.' How many people are, and have been, persecuted for fighting for justice!

Homily at Domus Sanctae Marthae, 9 June 2014

———

We are saved, which is why we are persecuted!

God has redeemed us. He has chosen us out of pure grace. With his death and resurrection he has redeemed us of the power of the world, of the power of the devil, of the power of the prince of this world. The origin of his hatred is this: we are saved and the prince of the world, who does not want us to be saved, hates us and brings into being the persecution that has continued from the first days of Jesus until today. Many Christian communities are persecuted in the world. Right now even more than at the start of Christianity! Today, now, on this day, at this time. Why? Because the spirit of the world is filled with hatred.

Homily at Domus Sanctae Marthae, 4 May 2013

Make definitive and radical choices

Entrusting oneself to the Lord's faithfulness is a choice that we too have the opportunity to make in our Christian lives. This involves a great and difficult decision. Throughout the history of the Church, and even in our own times, there are men and women, young and old, who make this decision. We realize it when we read the lives of the martyrs, when we read in the news about the persecution of Christians today. Let us think about our brothers and sisters who find themselves in extreme situations and who make this decision. They live in our own day and are examples for us. They encourage us to give the Church our whole livelihood.

Homily at Domus Sanctae Marthae, 25 November 2013

———

Make a revolution of happiness, against the dominant thought

The Beatitudes of Jesus are new and revolutionary. They present a model of happiness contrary to what is usually communicated by the media and by the prevailing wisdom. A worldly way of thinking finds it scandalous that God became one of us and died on a cross! According to the logic of this world, those whom Jesus proclaimed blessed are regarded as useless, 'losers'. What is glorified is success at any cost, affluence, the arrogance of power and self-affirmation at the expense of others.

Message for World Youth Day, 21 January 2014

Your Christian identity card

The Beatitudes are in some sense the Christian's *identity card*. They identify us as followers of Jesus. We are called to be blessed, to be followers of Jesus, to confront the troubles and anxieties of our age with the spirit and love of Jesus. Thus we ought to be able to recognize and respond to new situations with fresh spiritual energy. Blessed are those who remain faithful while enduring evils inflicted on them by others, and forgive them from their heart. Blessed are those who look into the eyes of the abandoned and marginalized, and show them their closeness. Blessed are those who see God in every person, and strive to make others also discover him. Blessed are those who protect and care for our common home. Blessed are those who renounce their own comfort in order to help others. Blessed are those who pray and work for full communion between Christians. All these are messengers of God's mercy and tenderness, and surely they will receive from him their merited reward.

Homily, 1 November 2016

FREE AND LIBERATED PEOPLE

'Take great care of your spiritual life, which is the source of inner freedom. Without prayer there is no inner freedom.'

6 June 2013

———

Liberate yourself from the power of things

Try to be *free with regard to material things*. The Lord calls us to a Gospel lifestyle marked by sobriety, by a refusal to yield to the culture of consumerism. This means being concerned with the essentials and learning to do without all those unneeded extras which hem us in. Let us learn to be detached from possessiveness and from the idolatry of money and lavish spending. Let us put Jesus first. He can free us from the kinds of idol-worship that enslave us. Put your trust in God, dear young friends! He knows and loves us, and he never forgets us. Just as he provides for the lilies of the field (cf. *Mt* 6:28), so he will make sure that we lack nothing. If we are to come through the financial crisis, we must also be ready to change our lifestyle and avoid so much wastefulness. Just as we need the courage to be happy, we also need the courage to live simply.

Message for World Youth Day, 21 January 2014

———

Go beyond the calculations of human efficiency

Finally, it is important to let the Gospel teach us the way of proclamation. At times, even with the best intentions, we can indulge in a certain hunger for power, proselytism or intolerant fanaticism. Yet the Gospel tells us to reject the idolatry of power and success, undue concern for structures, and a kind of anxiety that has more to do with the spirit of conquest than that of service. The seed of the kingdom, however tiny, unseen and at times insignificant, silently continues to grow, thanks to God's tireless activity. 'The kingdom of God is as if a man should scatter seed on the ground, and should sleep or rise night and day, and the seed should sprout and grow, he knows not how' (*Mk* 4:26–27). This is our first reason for confidence: God surpasses all our expectations and constantly surprises us by his generosity. He makes our efforts bear fruit beyond all human calculation.

Message for the World Day of Prayer for Vocations, 2017

Stop sitting at the table of slavery

On our existential journey there is always a tendency to resist liberation; we are afraid of freedom and, paradoxically and somewhat unwittingly, we prefer slavery. Freedom frightens us because it causes us to confront time and to face our responsibility to live it well. Instead, slavery reduces time to a 'moment' and thus we feel more secure; that is, it makes us live moments disconnected from their past and from our future. In other words, slavery impedes us from truly and fully living in the present, because it empties it of the past and closes it to the future, to eternity. Slavery makes us believe that we cannot dream, fly, hope.

A few days ago a great Italian artist said that it was easier for the Lord to take the Israelites out of Egypt than to take Egypt out of the heart of the Israelites. Yes, they were 'physically' freed from slavery, but during the wandering in the desert, with the various difficulties and the hunger, they began to feel nostalgia for Egypt and they remembered when they ate the onions and the garlic (cf. *Num* 11:5); they forgot, however, that they ate them at the table of slavery. Nostalgia for slavery is nestled in our heart, because it is seemingly more reassuring than freedom, which is far more risky. How we like being captivated by lots of fireworks, beautiful at first glance but which in reality last but a few seconds! This is the reign, this is the charm of the moment!

Homily, 31 December 2014

Be human because you are more than human

We become fully human when we become more than human, when we let God bring us beyond ourselves in order to attain the fullest truth of our being. Here we find the source and inspiration of all our efforts at evangelization. For if we have received the love that restores meaning to our lives, how can we fail to share that love with others?

Evangelii gaudium, 8

————

Make yourself free/free to give yourself

True freedom is always given by the Lord. Freedom first of all from sin, from selfishness in all its forms: freedom to give oneself and to do it with joy, like the Virgin of Nazareth who is free of herself, does not close in on herself in her condition – and she would indeed have had cause! – but thinks of those who in that moment are in greater need. She is free in the freedom of God, which is manifest in love. And this is the freedom that God has given to us, and we must not lose it: the freedom to adore God, to serve God and to serve him also in our brothers.

Homily, 5 July 2014

Do not be a slave to your personal goals

First of all it means being free from personal projects. Free from some of the tangible ways in which, perhaps, you may once have conceived of living your priesthood; from the possibility of planning your future; from the prospect of staying for any length of time in a place of 'your own' pastoral action. It means, in a certain way, making yourself free also with regard to the culture and mindset from which you come. This is not in order to forget it or even less to deny it, but rather to open yourselves in the charity of understanding different cultures and meeting people who belong to worlds far distant from your own.

Above all it means being alert to ensure you keep free of the ambitions or personal aims that can cause the Church great harm. You must be careful not to make either your own fulfilment or the recognition you might receive both inside and outside the ecclesiastical community a constant priority. Rather, your priority should be the loftier good of the Gospel cause and the accomplishment of the mission that will be entrusted to you. And I think this being free from ambitions or personal goals is important, it is important. Careerism is a form of leprosy, a leprosy. No careerism, please.

Address, 6 June 2013

God wants women and men without chains

God shows us that he is the good Father. And how does he do this? He does it through the incarnation of his Son, who becomes like one of us. Through this concrete man with the name Jesus we can understand God's true intention. He wants free human beings, because they always feel protected like the children of a good Father.

To achieve this plan, God only needs a human being. He needs a woman, a mother, to bring the Son into the world. She is the Virgin Mary, whom we honour with this Vespers celebration. Mary was completely free. In her freedom she said 'yes'. She did good forever. That way she served God and men and women. Let us imitate her example, if we want to know what God expects from his children.

Meeting, 5 August 2014

Always think about what you are doing

I would like to reflect on two fundamental values: freedom and service. First of all: be free people! What do I mean? Perhaps it is thought that freedom means doing everything one likes, or seeing how far one can go by trying drunkenness and overcoming boredom. This is not freedom. Freedom means being able to think about what we do, being able to assess what is good and what is bad, these are the types of conduct that lead to development; it means always opting for the good. Let us be free for goodness. And in this do not be afraid to go against the tide, even if it is not easy! Always being free to choose goodness is demanding but it will make you into people with a backbone who can face life, people with courage and patience (*parrhesia* and *ypomoné*).

Address, 7 June 2013

Worry is a good seed

When I hear that a young boy or girl is worried, I feel it is my duty to serve those young people, to provide a service for that worry, because that worry is like a seed, and then it will go on to bear fruit. And in that moment I feel that along with you I am providing a service to that which is the most precious at that moment, which is your worry.

Interview with young people, 31 March 2014

Receive the Commandments as a path towards your complete fulfilment

The Ten Commandments point to a path of freedom that finds fulfilment in the law of the Spirit that is written not on stone tables but on the heart (cf. 2 Cor 3:3): it is here that the Ten Commandments are written! It is fundamental to remember when God gave the Ten Commandments to the People of Israel through Moses. At the Red Sea the People had experienced great liberation; they had tangibly felt the power and faithfulness of God, of the God who sets us free. Now on Mount Sinai God himself points out to his People, and to all of us, the way to stay free, a way that is engraved in the human heart as a universal moral law (cf. *Ex* 20:1–17; *Dt* 5:1–22). We must not see the Ten Commandments as limitations of freedom – no, that is not what they are – but rather as signposts *to* freedom. They are not restrictions but indicators of freedom. They teach us to avoid the slavery to which we are condemned by so many idols that we ourselves build – we have experimented with them so often in history, and we are still experimenting with them today. They teach us to open ourselves to a broader dimension than that of the material, and to show people respect, overcoming the greed for power, for possessions, for money, in order to be honest and sincere in our relations, to protect the whole of creation and to nourish our planet with lofty, noble spiritual ideals. Following the Ten Commandments means being faithful to ourselves and to our most authentic nature, and walking towards the genuine freedom that Christ taught us in the Beatitudes.

Video message, 8 June 2013

Set out along the Trinitarian way

'Yes, Father, for such has been your gracious will' (*Lk* 10:21). These words of Jesus must be understood as referring to *his inner exultation.* The word 'gracious' describes the Father's saving and benevolent plan for humanity. It was this divine graciousness that made Jesus rejoice, for the Father willed to love people with the same love that he has for his Son. Luke also alludes to the similar exultation of Mary: 'My soul proclaims the greatness of the Lord, and my spirit exults in God my Saviour' (*Lk* 1:47). This is the Good News that leads to salvation. Mary, bearing in her womb Jesus, the evangelizer par excellence, met Elizabeth and rejoiced in the Holy Spirit as she sang her *Magnificat*. Jesus, seeing the success of his disciples' mission and their resulting joy, rejoiced in the Holy Spirit and addressed his Father in prayer. In both cases, it is joy for the working of salvation, for the love with which the Father loves his Son comes down to us, and through the Holy Spirit fills us and grants us a share in the Trinitarian life.

Message, 8 June 2014

It is God who sets us free

The Living God sets us free! Let us say 'yes' to love and not selfishness. Let us say 'yes' to life and not death. Let us say 'yes' to freedom and not enslavement to the many idols of our time. In a word, let us say 'yes' to the God who is love, life and freedom, and who never disappoints (cf. *1 Jn* 4:8, *Jn* 11:2, *Jn* 8:32); let us say 'yes' to the God who is the Living One and the Merciful One. Only faith in the Living

God saves us: in the God who in Jesus Christ has given us his own life by the gift of the Holy Spirit and has made it possible to live as true sons and daughters of God through his mercy. This faith brings us freedom and happiness.

Homily, 16 June 2013

Those who follow the Commandments say 'yes' to love

True freedom is not that of following our own selfishness, our blind passions; rather it is that of loving, of choosing what is good in every situation. The Ten Commandments are not a hymn to the 'no', they are to the 'yes'. A 'yes' to God, a 'yes' to Love, and since I say 'yes' to love, I say 'no' to non-love, but the 'no' is a consequence of that 'yes' that comes from God and makes us love.

Let us rediscover and live out the Ten Words of God! Let us say 'yes' to these 'ten paths of love', perfected by Christ, in order to defend human beings and direct them to true freedom!

Video message, 8 June 2013

Read God's signs in your life

Love Jesus Christ more and more! Our life is a response to his call and you will be happy and will build your life well if you can answer this call. May you feel the Lord's presence in your life. He is close to each one of you as a companion, as a friend who knows how to help and understand you, who encourages you in difficult times and never abandons you. In prayer, in conversation with him and in reading the Bible you will discover that he is truly close. You will also learn to read God's signs in your life. He always speaks to us, also through the events of our time and our daily life; it is up to us to listen to him.

Address, 7 June 2013

PART II

———

YOU AND OTHERS, HAPPINESS IN RELATIONSHIPS

BE INFECTIOUS LIGHT

'Receive and carry God's consolation: this mission is urgent.'
1 October 2016

———

The secret of a successful existence

The secret of a successful existence is to love and to give oneself for love. Then you find the strength to *'sacrifice yourself with joy'*, and the most involving commitment becomes the source of a greater joy. Then the definitive choices in life cease to be frightening, and appear in their true light, like a way of fully realizing one's own freedom.

Address, 21 April 2014

———

The service of others frees us from the sadness 'that casts us down'

This is the freedom which, by the grace of God, we experience in the Christian community, when we put ourselves at the service of one another. Without jealousy, impartially, without chatter . . . Serving one another, serving! Then, the Lord frees us of ambition and rivalry, which undermine unity and communion. He frees us from distrust, from sadness – this sadness is dangerous because it casts us down. It casts us down. It is dangerous. Be careful! He frees us from fear, from inner emptiness, isolation, regret and complaints. Even in our communities, in fact, there is no shortage of negative attitudes that make people self-referential, more concerned with defending themselves than with giving of themselves. But Christ frees us from this existential greyness, as we proclaimed in the Responsorial Psalm, 'You are my help and my deliverer'. For this reason, we disciples of the Lord, though still always weak and sinners – we are all so! – but although weak and sinners, we are called to live our faith with joy and courage, communion with God and with our brothers, in adoration of God, and to face with fortitude life's labours and trials.

Homily, 5 July 2014

———

Bring peace, bring the oil of Jesus

We are anointed: Christian means 'anointed'. And why are we anointed? To do what? 'He sent me to bring the good news.' To whom? 'To the poor, to bind up the brokenhearted, to proclaim liberty to the captives, and the opening of the prison to those who are bound; to proclaim the year of the Lord's favour' (cf. *Is* 61:1–2). This is the vocation of Christ and the vocation of Christians as well. To go to others, to those in need, whether their needs be material or spiritual . . . Many people who suffer anxiety because of family problems . . . To bring peace there, to bring the unction of Jesus, the oil of Jesus which does so much good and consoles souls.

Homily, 14 December 2014

––––––––

Happiness can't be bought

None of us knows what awaits us in life. And you young people: 'What awaits me?' We can do horrible, very horrible things, but please do not despair, there is always the Father there waiting for us! Come back, come back? That is the word. *Come back!* Come back home, because the Father is waiting for me there. And if I am a great sinner, there will be a big celebration. And you priests, please embrace the sinners and be merciful. And this is a beautiful feeling! This makes me happy, because God never tires of forgiving; he never tires of waiting for us.

Address, 15 August 2014

––––––––

With infectious joy: that is how the Gospel announces itself

When Jesus sent the Twelve out on mission, he said to them: take no gold, nor silver, nor copper in your belts, no bag for your journey, nor two tunics, nor sandals, nor a staff; for the labourers deserve their food (*Mt* 10:9–10). Evangelical poverty is a basic condition for spreading the kingdom of God. The most beautiful and spontaneous expressions of joy that I have seen during my life were by poor people who had little to hold on to. Evangelization in our time will only take place as the result of infectious joy.

Message for World Youth Day, 21 January 2014

Learn and teach discernment

When you are a child it is easy for your father and mother to tell you what we must do, and it is fine – today I don't think it's so easy; in my day it was, but today it isn't, and yet it's easier. But gradually we grow up surrounded by a multitude of voices, all of which seem to be right, the discernment of that which leads to resurrection, to life and not to a culture of death, is crucial. That is why I stress this necessity so firmly. It is a catechetic instrument, not least for life. In catechesis, in spiritual guidance, in homilies, we must teach our people, teach the young, teach children discernment. And teach them to ask for the grace of discernment.

Address, 25 March 2017

Christ is knocking at the door of your heart today.
Knock at your brothers' and sisters' hearts as well.

Today Christ is knocking at the door of your heart, and my heart as well. He is calling me and you to stand up, to be fully awake and alert, to see the things in life that really matter. And even more than that, he asks you and me to walk the streets and paths of this world and knock at the door of other people's hearts, inviting them to welcome him into their lives.

Address, 15 August 2014

———

Those who love the poor fulfil the Gospel (not Communism)

I am a believer; I believe in God; I believe in Jesus Christ and in his Gospel, and the heart of the Gospel is the proclamation to the poor. When you read the Beatitudes, for instance, or you read Matthew 25, you see there how clear Jesus is about this. This is the heart of the Gospel. And Jesus says of himself: 'I have come to proclaim freedom to the poor, salvation, the grace of God . . .' – to the poor. Those who are in need of salvation, who are in need of being received in society. Then, if you read the Gospel, you see that Jesus had a certain preference for the marginalized: the lepers, the widows, orphan children, the blind . . . marginalized persons. And also great sinners . . . and this is my consolation! Yes, because he is not even alarmed by sin! When he met a person like Zacchaeus, who was a thief, or like Matthew, who was a traitor to the homeland for money, he wasn't frightened! He looked at him and chose him. This is also poverty: the poverty of sin. For me, the poor are the heart of the Gospel. I heard, two months ago, that a person said, because of this talk of the poor, because of this preference: 'This Pope is a Communist.' No! This is a banner of the Gospel, not of Communism – of the Gospel! However, it's poverty without ideology, poverty . . . And, therefore, I believe that the poor are the centre of Jesus' proclamation.

Interview with young people, 31 March 2014

———

Recognize others and seek your own good

Goodness always tends to spread. Every authentic experience of truth and goodness seeks by its very nature to grow within us, and any person who has experienced a profound liberation becomes more sensitive to the needs of others. As it expands, goodness takes root and develops. If we wish to lead a dignified and fulfilling life, we have to reach out to others and seek their good.

Evangelii gaudium, 9

———

True joy is born from encounters

We know that all this can satisfy some desires or create some emotions, but in the end it is a joy that stays on the surface, it does not sink to the depths, it is not an intimate joy: it is momentary tipsiness that does not make us really happy. Joy is not transitory tipsiness: it is something quite different!

True joy does not come from things or from possessing, no! It is born from the encounter, from the relationship with others, it is born from feeling accepted, understood and loved, and from accepting, from understanding and from loving; and this is not because of a passing fancy but because the other is a person. Joy is born from the gratuitousness of an encounter! It is hearing someone say, but not necessarily with words: 'You are important to me'. This is beautiful . . . And it is these very words that God makes us understand. In calling you, God says to you: 'You are important to me, I love you, I am counting on you'. Jesus says this to each one of us! Joy is born from that! The joy of the moment in which Jesus looked at me. Understanding and hearing this is the secret of our joy. Feeling loved by God, feeling that for him we are not numbers but people; and hearing him calling us. Becoming a priest or a religious man or woman is not primarily our own decision. I do not trust that seminarian or that woman novice who says: 'I have chosen this path'. I do not like this! It won't do! Rather it is the response to a call and to a call of love. I hear something within me that moves me and I answer 'yes'. It is in prayer that the Lord makes us understand this love, but it is also through so many signs that we can read in our life, in the many people he sets on our path. And the joy of the encounter with him and with his call does

not lead to shutting oneself in but to opening oneself; it leads
to service in the Church.

Meeting with seminarians and novices, 6 July 2013

Dry your own tears, and your brothers' and sisters' tears

Another face of mercy is *consolation*. 'Comfort, comfort my
people' (*Is* 40:1) is the heartfelt plea that the prophet continues to make today, so that a word of hope may come to all those
who experience suffering and pain. Let us never allow ourselves to be robbed of the hope born of faith in the Risen Lord.
True, we are often sorely tested, but we must never lose our
certainty of the Lord's love for us. His mercy finds expression
also in the closeness, affection and support that many of our
brothers and sisters can offer us at times of sadness and affliction. The drying of tears is one way to break the vicious circle
of solitude in which we often find ourselves trapped.

Misericordia et misera, 13

Go towards the poor, do not fill your mouth with their name

All of us need to experience *a conversion in the way we see the poor*.
We have to care for them and be sensitive to their spiritual
and material needs. To you young people I especially entrust
the task of restoring solidarity to the heart of human culture.
Faced with old and new forms of poverty – unemployment,

migration and addictions of various kinds – we have the duty to be alert and thoughtful, avoiding the temptation to remain indifferent. We have to remember all those who feel unloved, who have no hope for the future and who have given up on life out of discouragement, disappointment or fear. We have to learn to be on the side of the poor, and not just indulge in rhetoric about the poor! Let us go out to meet them, look into their eyes and listen to them. The poor provide us with a concrete opportunity to encounter Christ himself, and to touch his suffering flesh.

Message for World Youth Day, 21 January 2014

———

At the end of everything, what is left? God and other people!

Today God questions us about the meaning of our lives. Using an image, we could say that these readings serve as a 'strainer' through which our life can be poured: they remind us that almost everything in this world is passing away, like running water. But there are treasured realities that remain, like a precious stone in a strainer. What endures, what has value in life, what riches do not disappear? Surely these two: *the Lord and our neighbour*. These two riches do not disappear! These are the greatest goods; these are to be loved. Everything else – the heavens, the earth, all that is most beautiful, even this Basilica – will pass away; but we must never exclude *God or others* from our lives.

Homily, 13 November 2016

Where is your treasure?

'Where is your treasure? In what does your heart find its rest?' Yes, our hearts can be attached to true or false treasures, they can find genuine rest or they can simply slumber, becoming lazy and lethargic. The greatest good we can have in life is our relationship with God. Are you convinced of this? Do you realize how much you are worth in the eyes of God? Do you know that you are loved and welcomed by him unconditionally, as indeed you are? Once we lose our sense of this, we human beings become an incomprehensible enigma, for it is the knowledge that we are loved unconditionally by God that gives meaning to our lives. Do you remember the conversation that Jesus had with the rich young man (cf. *Mk* 10:17–22)? The evangelist Mark observes that the Lord looked upon him and loved him (v. 21), and invited him to follow him and thus to find true riches.

Message for World Youth Day, 31 January 2015

Where does your heart find rest?

The question I would like to ask you is not an original one. I take it from the Gospel. But I think that having heard you, perhaps it is the right moment for you. Where is your treasure? That is the question. Where does your heart find rest? On what treasure does your heart rest? Because where your treasure is, your life will be. The heart is attached to the treasure, to a treasure that we all have: power, money, pride, so many things . . . or goodness, beauty, the desire to do good . . . There can be so many treasures. Where is your treasure? That is the question I will put to you, but you will have to give the answer to yourselves, on your own! At home . . .

Interview with young people, 31 March 2014

―――――

Choose the woman and the man you want to be: selfish or fraternal

An authentic spirit of fraternity overcomes the individual selfishness which conflicts with people's ability to live in freedom and in harmony among themselves. Such selfishness develops socially − whether it is in the many forms of corruption, so widespread today, or in the formation of criminal organizations, from small groups to those organized on a global scale. These groups tear down legality and justice, striking at the very heart of the dignity of the person. These organizations gravely offend God, they hurt others and they harm creation, all the more so when they have religious overtones.

I also think of the heartbreaking tragedy of drug abuse, which reaps profits in contempt of the moral and civil laws. I think of the devastation of natural resources and ongoing pollution, and the tragedy of the exploitation of labour. I think, too, of illicit money trafficking and financial speculation, which often prove both predatory and harmful for entire economic and social systems, exposing millions of men and women to poverty. I think of prostitution, which every day reaps innocent victims, especially the young, robbing them of their future. I think of the abomination of human trafficking, crimes and abuses against minors, the horror of slavery still present in many parts of the world; the frequently overlooked tragedy of migrants, who are often victims of disgraceful and illegal manipulation.

Message for World Day of Peace, 2014

Learn from the wisdom of the poor

The poor are not just people to whom we can give something. They have *much to offer us and to teach us.* How much we have to learn from the wisdom of the poor! Think about it: several hundred years ago a saint, Benedict Joseph Labré, who lived on the streets of Rome from the alms he received, became a spiritual guide to all sorts of people, including nobles and prelates. In a very real way, the poor are our teachers. They show us that people's value is not measured by their possessions or how much money they have in the bank. A poor person, a person lacking material possessions, always maintains his or her dignity. The poor can teach us much about humility and trust in God. In the parable of the pharisee and the tax collector (cf. *Lk* 18:9–14), Jesus holds the tax collector up as a model because of his humility and his acknowledgment that he is a sinner. The widow who gave her last two coins to the temple treasury is an example of the generosity of all those who have next to nothing and yet give away everything they have (*Lk* 21:1–4).

Message for World Youth Day, 21 January 2014

Let the Church be the home of your consolation

God does not console us only in our hearts; through the prophet Isaiah he adds: 'You shall be comforted in Jerusalem' (66:13). In Jerusalem, that is, in the city of God, in the community: it is when we are united, in communion, that God's consolation works in us. In the Church we find consolation, it is *the house of consolation*: here God wishes to console us. We may ask ourselves: I who am in the Church, do I bring the consolation of God? Do I know how to welcome others as guests and console those whom I see tired and disillusioned? Even when enduring affliction and rejection, a Christian is always called to bring hope to the hearts of those who have given up, to encourage the downhearted, to bring the light of Jesus, the warmth of his presence and his forgiveness which restores us. Countless people suffer trials and injustice, and live in anxiety. Our hearts need anointing with God's consolation, which does not take away our problems, but gives us the power to love, to endure pain in peace.

Homily, 1 October 2016

In dialogue, the path towards God

Q. (*girl*): I see God in other people. Where do you see God?
A. (*Pope Francis*): I try, I try . . . to meet him in every circumstance of life. I try . . . I find him in my reading of the Bible, I find him in the celebration of the Sacraments, I try to find him in prayer and also in my work, in people, in various people . . . Above all I find him in the sick: the sick do me good, because I wonder, when I am with a sick person, why him and not me? And I find him with prisoners: why is he imprisoned and I'm not? And I talk to God: 'You always perform an injustice: why him and not me?' And I find God in this, but always in dialogue. It does me good to try to find him throughout the whole day. I can't do it, but I try to do that, to be in dialogue. I can't do it like this: the saints did it well, I don't yet . . . But this is the path.

Interview with young people, 31 March 2014

We all need comfort

All of us need consolation because no one is spared suffering, pain and misunderstanding. How much pain can be caused by a spiteful remark born of envy, jealousy or anger! What great suffering is caused by the experience of betrayal, violence and abandonment! How much sorrow in the face of the death of a loved one! And yet God is never far from us at these moments of sadness and trouble. A reassuring word, an embrace that makes us feel understood, a caress that makes us experience love, a prayer that makes us stronger . . . all these things express God's closeness through the consolation offered by our brothers and sisters.

Misericordia et misera, 13

———

We are reflections of a transforming light

Jesus invites us to be a reflection of his light, by witnessing with good works. He says: 'Let your light so shine before men, that they may see your good works and give glory to your Father who is in heaven' (*Mt* 5:16). These words emphasize that we are recognizable as true disciples of the One who is the Light of the World, not in words, but by our works. Indeed, it is above all our behaviour that – good or bad – leaves a mark on others. Therefore, we have a duty and a responsibility towards the gift received: the light of the faith, which is in us through Christ and the action of the Holy Spirit; and we must not withhold it as if it were our property. Instead we are called to make it shine throughout the world, to offer it to others through good works. How much the world needs the light of the Gospel which transforms, heals and guarantees salvation to those who receive it! We must convey this light through our good works.

Angelus, 5 February 2017

A smile will change your life

Let us ask ourselves, as individuals and as communities, whether we feel challenged when, in our daily lives, we meet or deal with persons who could be victims of human trafficking, or when we are tempted to select items that may well have been produced by exploiting others. Some of us, out of indifference, or for financial reasons, or because we are caught up in our daily concerns, close our eyes to this. Others, however, decide to do something about it, to join civic associations or to practise small, everyday gestures — which have so much merit! — such as offering a kind word, a greeting or a smile. These cost us nothing but they can offer hope, open doors, and change the life of another person who lives clandestinely; they can also change our own lives with respect to this reality.

Message for the World Day of Peace, 2015

———

Your compassion can come about even in silence

Sometimes, too, *silence* can be helpful, especially when we cannot find words in response to the questions of those who suffer. A lack of words, however, can be made up for by the compassion of a person who stays at our side, who loves us and who holds out a hand. It is not true that silence is an act of surrender; on the contrary, it is a moment of strength and love. Silence, too, belongs to our language of consolation, because it becomes a concrete way of sharing in the suffering of a brother or sister.

Misericordia et misera, 13

———

In communion with love

It is not enough to know that God is born, if you do not celebrate with him *Christmas in the heart*. God is born, yes, but is he born in your heart? Is he born in my heart? Is he born in our hearts? And in this way we will find him, as did the Magi, with Mary and Joseph in the stable.

The Magi went forth: having found the Child, 'they fell down and worshipped him' (*Mt* 2:11). They did not just look at him, they did not just say a generic prayer and leave, no indeed, *they worshipped*: they entered into a personal communion of love with Jesus.

Angelus, 6 January 2017

———

We are the salt that gives flavour

The light of our faith, in giving of oneself, does not fade but strengthens. However, it can weaken if we do not nourish it with love and with charitable works. [. . .]

Thus, Christians' mission in society is that of giving 'flavour' to life with the faith and the love that Christ has given us, and at the same time, keeping away the contaminating seeds of selfishness, envy, slander and so on. [. . .]

Each one of us is called to be *light and salt*, in the environment of our daily life, persevering in the task of regenerating the human reality in the spirit of the Gospel and in the perspective of the kingdom of God.

Angelus, 5 February 2017

————

Like water in beans

It is important to be able to make people welcome; this is something even more beautiful than any kind of ornament or decoration. I say this because when we are generous in welcoming people and sharing something with them – some food, a place in our homes, our time – not only do we no longer remain poor: we are enriched. I am well aware that when someone needing food knocks at your door, you always find a way of sharing food; as the proverb says, one can always 'add more water to the beans'! Is it possible to add more water to the beans? . . . Always? . . . And you do so with love, demonstrating that true riches consist not in material things, but in the heart!

Address, 25 July 2013

Goodness pays more than money

Differences do not impede harmony, joy and peace, in fact they become the opportunity for a deeper reciprocal knowledge and understanding. Different religious experiences open up to respectful and effective love towards one's neighbours; every religious community is expressed with love and not with violence, don't be ashamed of goodness! To those who let it grow within them, goodness gives a calm consciousness, a deep joy not least amid difficulties and incomprehension. Even when confronted with sudden offences, goodness is not weakness, but true strength, capable of renouncing revenge.

Goodness is its own reward and brings us closer to God, the Supreme Good. It makes us think like him, it makes us see the reality of our life in the light of his plan of love for each one of us, it makes us savour small everyday joys and sustains us in our difficulties and trials. Goodness pays infinitely more than money, which disappoints because we were created to receive the love of God and give it away in turn, not to measure everything on the basis of money or power, which is the danger that kills us all.

Address, 21 April 2014

———

Granting forgiveness is not like giving alms

Forgiveness is possible. The wound can heal, can be healed; the wound closes up. But often the scar remains. And this means:

'I cannot forget, but I have forgiven'. Always, forgiveness. But not going to that person to give forgiveness as if I were giving alms, no. Forgiveness is born in the heart and I begin to treat that person as if nothing had happened . . . A smile, and slowly forgiveness comes. Forgiveness is not given by decree: it needs an inner journey on our part, to forgive. It is not easy . . .

Interview with children and young people, 15 January 2017

Granting hope needs a body to support it

Hope, to be nourished, *necessarily needs a 'body'*, in which the various members support and revive each other. This means, then, that if we hope, it is because many of our brothers and sisters have taught us to hope and have kept our hope alive. Distinguishable among these are *the little ones, the poor, the simple* and *the marginalized*. Yes, because one who is enclosed within his own wellbeing does not know hope: he hopes only in his wellbeing and this is not hope: it is relative security; one who is enclosed in his own fulfilment, who always feels that all is well, does not know hope. Instead, those who hope are those who each day experience trials, precariousness and their own limitations. These brothers and sisters of ours give us the strongest, most beautiful witness, because they stand firm, trusting in the Lord, knowing that, beyond the sadness, oppression and inevitability of death, the last word will be his, and it will be a word of mercy, of life and of peace. Whoever hopes, hopes to one day hear this word: 'Come, come to me, brother; come, come to me, sister, for all eternity'.

General audience, 8 February 2017

To have a full life: stimulate, don't just punish

I remember once at school there was a pupil who was a phenomenon at playing football and a disaster when it came to behaviour in the classroom. One rule I'd given him was that if he didn't behave well he would have to give up football, which he liked so much! Since he went on misbehaving he spent two months without playing, and that made things worse. Be careful when you punish people: that boy got worse. It's true, I knew that boy. One day the coach spoke to the headmistress and explained: 'This isn't working! Let me try,' he said to the headmistress, and asked if the boy could start playing again. 'Let's try,' she said. And the coach made him captain of the team. Well that child, that boy, felt he'd been treated considerately, he felt he could give his best and not only stopped behaving badly, but his overall school performance improved. That strikes me as very important in education. Very important. Among our students there are some who are keen on sport and not so much on the sciences, while others are better at art than maths, and others better at philosophy than sport. A good teacher, educator or coach knows how to stimulate the good qualities of his pupils and not neglect the others.

Address, 25 March 2017

Blessed be your community too

Blessed are those Christian communities who live this authentic Gospel simplicity! Poor in means, they are rich in God. Blessed are the Shepherds who do not ride the logic of worldly success, but follow the law of love: welcoming, listening, serving. Blessed is the Church who does not entrust herself to the criteria of functionalism and organizational efficiency, nor worries about her image.

Homily, 1 October 2016

———

Live as one who is reconciled

The reconciled person sees in God the Father of all, and, as a consequence, is spurred on to live a life of fraternity open to all. In Christ, the other is welcomed and loved as a son or daughter of God, as a brother or sister, not as a stranger, much less as a rival or even an enemy. In God's family, where all are sons and daughters of the same Father, and, because they are grafted to Christ, *sons and daughters in the Son*, there are no 'disposable lives'. All men and women enjoy an equal and inviolable dignity.

Message for the World Day of Peace, 2014

THE FAMILY,
THE FULFILMENT OF LIFE

'I need to rest in the Lord with the family, and remember my family: my
father, my mother, my grandmother, my grandfather . . .'
16 January 2015

———

The anxiety of the solitary man

In speaking of marriage, Jesus refers us to yet another page
of Genesis, which, in its second chapter, paints a splendid
and detailed portrait of the couple. First, we see the man,
who anxiously seeks 'a helper fit for him' (vv. 18, 20), capable of alleviating the solitude that he feels amid the animals
and the world around him. The original Hebrew suggests a
direct encounter, face to face, eye to eye, in a kind of silent
dialogue, for where love is concerned, silence is always more
eloquent than words. It is an encounter with a face, a 'thou',
who reflects God's own love and is man's 'best possession, a
helper fit for him and a pillar of support', in the words of
the biblical sage (*Sir* 36:24). Or again, as the woman of the

Song of Solomon will sing in a magnificent profession of love and mutual self-bestowal: 'My beloved is mine and I am his . . . I am my beloved's and my beloved is mine' (2:16, 6:3).

This encounter, which relieves man's solitude, gives rise to new birth and to the family.

Amoris Laetitia, 12

———

Does your family still dream?

I am very fond of dreams in families. For nine months every mother and father dreams about their baby. Am I right? [Yes!] They dream about what kind of child he or she will be . . . You can't have a family without dreams. Once a family loses the ability to dream, children do not grow, love does not grow, life shrivels up and dies. So I ask you each evening, when you make your examination of conscience, to also ask yourselves this question: Today did I dream about my children's future? Today did I dream about the love of my husband, my wife? Did I dream about my parents and grandparents who have gone before me? Dreaming is very important. Especially dreaming in families. Do not lose this ability to dream!

Address, 16 January 2015

Human fulfilment 'in one flesh'

Adam, who is also the man of every time and place, together with his wife, starts a new family. Jesus speaks of this by quoting the passage from Genesis: 'The man shall be joined to his wife, and the two shall become one' (*Mt* 19:5; cf. *Gen* 2:24). The very words 'to be joined' or 'to cleave', in the original Hebrew, bespeaks a profound harmony, a closeness both physical and interior, to such an extent that the word is used to describe our union with God: 'My soul clings to you' (*Ps* 63:8). The marital union is thus evoked not only in its sexual and corporal dimension, but also in its voluntary self-giving in love. The result of this union is that the two 'become one flesh', both physically and in the union of their hearts and lives, and, eventually, in a child, who will share not only genetically but also spiritually in the 'flesh' of both parents.

Amoris Laetitia, 13

Make love 'normal'

Each Christian family can first of all – as Mary and Joseph did – welcome Jesus, listen to him, speak with him, guard him, protect him, grow with him; and in this way improve the world. Let us make room in our heart and in our day for the Lord. As Mary and Joseph also did, and it was not easy: how many difficulties they had to overcome! They were not a superficial family, they were not an unreal family. The family of Nazareth urges us to rediscover the vocation and mission of the family, of every family. And, what happened in those thirty years in Nazareth can thus happen to us too: in seeking to make love and not hate normal, making mutual help commonplace, not indifference or enmity.

General audience, 17 December 2014

———

Do not reduce dedication to others to a provision of services

Freedom of choice makes it possible to plan our lives and to make the most of ourselves. Yet if this freedom lacks noble goals or personal discipline, it degenerates into an inability to give oneself generously to others. Indeed, in many countries where the number of marriages is decreasing, more and more people are choosing to live alone or simply to spend time together without cohabiting. We can also point to a praiseworthy concern for justice; but if misunderstood, this can turn citizens into clients interested solely in the provision of services.

Amoris Laetitia, 33

———

Families, come to me and I will give you rest!

Dear families, the Lord knows our struggles: he knows them. He knows the burdens we have in our lives. But the Lord also knows our great desire to find joy and rest! Do you remember? Jesus said, '... *that your joy may be complete*' (cf. *Jn* 15:11). Jesus wants our joy to be complete! He said this to the Apostles and today he says it to us. Here, then, is the first thing I would like to share with you this evening, and it is a saying of Jesus: Come to me, families from around the world – Jesus says – and I will give you rest, so that your joy may be complete. Take home this Word of Jesus, carry it in your hearts, share it with the family. It invites us to come to Jesus so that he may give this joy to us and to everyone.

Address, 26 October 2013

———

Rediscover the joy of embraces

In the family, we learn to embrace and support one another, to discern the meaning of facial expressions and moments of silence, to laugh and cry together with people who did not choose one another yet are so important to each other. This greatly helps us to understand the meaning of communication as *recognizing and creating closeness*. When we lessen distances by growing closer and accepting one another, we experience gratitude and joy. Mary's greeting and the stirring of her child are a blessing for Elizabeth; they are followed by the beautiful canticle of the *Magnificat*, in which Mary praises God's loving plan for her and for her people. A 'yes' spoken with faith can have effects that go well beyond ourselves and our place in the world.

Message, 23 January 2015

The family that prays together stays together

Resting in prayer is especially important for families. It is in the family that we first learn how to pray. Don't forget: the family that prays together stays together! This is important. There we come to know God, to grow into men and women of faith, to see ourselves as members of God's greater family, the Church. In the family we learn how to love, to forgive, to be generous and open, not closed and selfish. We learn to move beyond our own needs, to encounter others and share our lives with them. That is why it is so important to pray as a family! So important! That is why families are so important in God's plan for the Church! To rest in the Lord is to pray. To pray together as a family.

Address, 16 January 2015

———

There is no perfect family: turn it into a school of forgiveness

More than anywhere else, the family is where we daily experience our own *limits* and those of others, the problems great and small entailed in living peacefully with others. A perfect family does not exist. We should not be fearful of imperfections, weakness or even conflict, but rather learn how to deal with them constructively. The family, where we keep loving one another despite our limits and sins, thus becomes a *school of forgiveness*.

Message, 23 January 2015

Tell young married couples their love is beautiful!

Spousal and familial love also clearly reveals the vocation of the person to love in a unique way and forever, and that the trials, sacrifices and crises of couples as well as of the family as a whole represent pathways for growth in goodness, truth and beauty. In marriage we give ourselves completely without calculation or reserve, sharing everything, gifts and hardship, trusting in God's Providence. This is the experience that the young can learn from their parents and grandparents. It is an experience of faith in God and of mutual trust, profound freedom and holiness, because holiness presumes giving oneself with fidelity and sacrifice every day of one's life! But there are problems in marriage. Always different points of view, jealousy, arguing. But we need to say to young spouses that they should never end the day without making peace. The Sacrament of marriage is renewed in this act of peace after an argument, a misunderstanding, a hidden jealousy, even a sin. Making peace gives unity to the family; and tell young people, young couples, that it is not easy to go down this path, but it is a very beautiful path, very beautiful. You need to tell them!

Address, 25 October 2013

———

Don't turn the Gospel into dead stones to hurl at the poor

I would like to mention the situation of families living in dire poverty and great limitations. The problems faced by poor households are often all the more trying. For example, if a single mother has to raise a child by herself and needs to leave the child alone at home while she goes to work, the child can grow up exposed to all kind of risks and obstacles to personal growth. In such difficult situations of need, the Church must be particularly concerned to offer understanding, comfort and acceptance, rather than imposing straight away a set of rules that only leads people to feel judged and abandoned by the very Mother called to show them God's mercy. Rather than offering the healing power of grace and the light of the Gospel message, some would 'indoctrinate' that message, turning it into 'dead stones to be hurled at others'.

Amoris Laetitia, 49

A family that teaches goodness is a blessing to the world

When families bring children into the world, train them in faith and sound values, and teach them to contribute to society, they become a blessing in our world. Families can become a blessing for all of humanity! God's love becomes present and active by the way we love and by the good works that we do. We extend Christ's kingdom in this world. And in doing this, we prove faithful to the prophetic mission which we have received in Baptism.

Address, 16 January 2015

The importance of walking united

Sometimes I think of marriages that separate after many years. 'Well . . . no, we're not getting on, we've grown apart.' Perhaps they didn't know how to ask for forgiveness in time. Perhaps they didn't know how to forgive in time. And I always give this advice to newlyweds: 'Argue as much as you like. If the plates fly, let them. But never end the day without making peace. Never!' And if the couple learn to say, 'Sorry, I was tired' or just a little gesture: this is peace; and resume their normal life the next day. This is a lovely secret, and avoids those painful separations. How important it is to walk united, without headlong rushes, without nostalgia for the past. And while you walk you talk, you get to know each other, you tell each other stories, you grow into a family. Here we ask ourselves: how are we walking?

Address, 4 October 2013

———

How beautiful is the richness of relationships between men and women!

The most beautiful family, a protagonist and not a problem, is the one that is able to *communicate*, starting from *witness*, the beauty and richness of the relationship between man and woman, and the one between parents and children. We don't fight to defend the past, but we work with patience and trust, in all the environments that we live in every day, to build the future.

Message, 23 January 2015

The mission of your family is to 'make room for Jesus in the world'

'Nazareth' means 'she who keeps', as Mary, who – as the Gospel states – 'kept all these things in her heart' (cf. *Lk* 2:19, 51). Since then, each time there is a family that keeps this mystery, even if it were on the periphery of the world, the mystery of the Son of God, the mystery of Jesus who comes to save us, the mystery is at work. He comes to save the world. And this is the great mission of the family: to make room for Jesus who is coming, to welcome Jesus into the family, in each member: children, husband, wife, grandparents . . . Jesus is there. Welcome him there, in order that he grow spiritually in the family.

General audience, 17 December 2014

———

Your womb, your bond, your tongue . . .

Even after we have come into the world, in some sense we are still in a 'womb', which is the family. *A womb made up of various interrelated persons*: the family is 'where we learn to live with others despite our differences' (*Evangelii gaudium*, 66). Notwithstanding the differences of gender and age between them, family members accept one another because there is a bond between them. The wider the range of these relationships and the greater the differences of age, the richer will be our living environment. It is this *bond* that is at the root of *language*, which in turn strengthens the bond. We do not create our language; we can use it because we have received it. It is in the family that we learn to speak our *'mother tongue'*, the language of those who have gone before us. (cf. *2 Macc* 7:25, 27). In the family we realize that others have preceded us; they made it possible for us to exist and in our turn to generate life and to do something good and beautiful. We can give because we have received. This virtuous circle is at the heart of the family's ability to communicate among its members and with others. More generally, it is the model for all communication.

Message, 23 January 2015

––––––

When the joy of the young meets the consolation of the old

Four times Our Lady and Saint Joseph *wanted to do what was required by the Law of the Lord* (cf. *Lk* 2:22, 23, 24, 27). One almost feels and perceives that Jesus' parents have the joy of observing the precepts of God, yes, the joy of walking according to the Law of the Lord! They are two newlyweds, they have just had their baby, and they are motivated by the desire to do what is prescribed. This is not an external fact; it is not just to feel right, no! It's a strong desire, a deep desire, full of joy. That's what the Psalm says: 'In the way of thy testimonies I delight . . . For thy law is my delight' (119 [118]:14, 77).

And what does Saint Luke say of the elderly? He underlines, more than once, that *they were guided by the Holy Spirit*. He says Simeon was a righteous and devout man, awaiting the consolation of Israel, and that 'the Holy Spirit was upon him' (2:25). He says that 'it had been revealed to him by the Holy

Spirit that he should not see death before he had seen the Lord's Christ' (v. 26); and finally that he went to the Temple 'inspired by the Spirit' (v. 27). He says Anna was a 'prophet-ess' (v. 36); that is she was inspired by God and that she was always 'worshipping with fasting and prayer' in the Temple (v. 37). In short, these two elders are full of life! They are full of life because they are enlivened by the Holy Spirit, obedient to his action, sensitive to his calls . . .

And now there is the encounter between the Holy Family and the two representatives of the holy people of God. Jesus is at the centre. It is he who moves everything, who draws all of them to the Temple, the house of his Father.

It is a meeting between the young, who are full of joy in observing the Law of the Lord, and the elderly who are full of joy in the action of the Holy Spirit. It is *a unique encounter between observance and prophecy*, where young people are the observers and the elderly are prophets! In fact, if we think carefully, observance of the Law is animated by the Spirit and the prophecy moves forward along the path traced by the Law. Who, more than Mary, is full of the Holy Spirit? Who more than she is docile to its action?

Homily, 2 February 2014

———

Visit, open doors, don't close yourself up, bring comfort . . .

To 'visit' is to open doors, not remaining closed in our little world, but rather going out to others. So too the family comes alive as it reaches beyond itself; families who do so communicate their message of life and communion, giving comfort and hope to more fragile families, and thus build up the Church herself, which is the family of families.

Message, 23 January 2015

————

Turn your family into a story of communion

The family is not a subject of debate or a terrain for ideological skirmishes. Rather, it is *an environment in which we learn to communicate* in an experience of closeness, a setting where communication takes place, a *'communicating community'*. The family is a community that provides help, that celebrates life and is fruitful. Once we realize this, we will once more be able to see how the family continues to be a rich human resource, as opposed to a problem or an institution in crisis. At times the *media* can tend to present the family as a kind of abstract model which has to be accepted or rejected, defended or attacked, rather than as a living reality. Or else as grounds for ideological clashes rather than as a setting where we can all learn what it means to communicate in a love received and returned. Relating our experiences means realizing that our lives are bound together as a single reality, that our voices are many, and that each is unique.

Message, 23 January 2015

SUCCESSFUL LIVES:
VOCATIONS LIVED WITH JOY

'Do not be afraid to show the joy of having replied to the call of the Lord, to his choice of love and to bear witness to his Gospel.'

6 July 2015

———

A gloomy disciple is a disciple of gloom

None of us should be dour, discontented and dissatisfied, for a gloomy disciple is a disciple of gloom. Like everyone else, we have our troubles, our dark nights of the soul, our disappointments and infirmities, our experience of slowing down as we grow older. But in all these things we should be able to discover 'perfect joy'. For it is here that we learn to recognize the face of Christ, who became like us in all things, and to rejoice in the knowledge that we are being conformed to him who, out of love of us, did not refuse the sufferings of the cross.

In a society that exalts the cult of efficiency, fitness and success, one that ignores the poor and dismisses 'losers', we

can witness by our lives to the truth of the words of Scripture: 'When I am weak, then I am strong' (2 *Cor* 12:10).

Letter to all consecrated people, 21 November 2014

The place where joy is born

I wanted to say a word to you and the word is 'joy'. Wherever
there are consecrated people, seminarians, priests and nuns,
young people, there is joy, there is always joy! It is the joy of
freshness, the joy of following Jesus; the joy that the Holy
Spirit gives us, not the joy of the world. There is joy! But –
where is joy born? It is born . . . but on Saturday evening shall
I be going home or will I go out dancing with my former
friends? Is joy born from this? For a seminarian, for example?
No? Or yes?

Meeting with seminarians and novices, 6 July 2013

Contagion and attraction

'The Church does not grow from proselytizing, but from
attraction'; this joy's testimony that proclaims Jesus Christ
attracts people. This witness born from the joy accepted and
then transformed into proclamation. It is the founding joy.
Without this joy, without this glee, we cannot found a
Church! We cannot establish a Christian community! It is an
apostolic joy, that radiates and expands. Like Peter, I ask

myself: 'Am I able, like Peter, to sit next to my brother and slowly explain the gift of the Word that I have received, and infect him with my joy? Am I capable of arousing around me the enthusiasm of those who discover in us the miracle of a new life, which cannot be controlled, which demands docility because it draws us, it carries us; and is this new life born from the encounter with Christ?'

Homily, 24 April 2014

———

The scent of the people and the name of the dog

What could be more beautiful for us than walking with our people? It is beautiful! When I think of the parish priests who knew the names of their parishioners, who went to visit them; even as one of them told me: 'I know the name of each family's dog'. They even knew the dog's name! How nice it was! What could be more beautiful than this? I repeat it often: walking with our people, sometimes in front, some- times in the middle, and sometimes behind: in front in order to guide the community, in the middle in order to encourage and support; and at the back in order to keep it united and so that no one lags too far behind, to keep them united. There is another reason, too: because the people have a 'nose'! The people scent out, discover, new ways to walk, it has the '*sensus fidei*,' as theologians call it. What could be more beautiful than this? During the Synod, it will be very important to consider what the Holy Spirit is saying to the laity, to the People of God, to everyone.

Address, 4 October 2013

————

Open your heart to great ideals

No vocation is born of itself or lives for itself. A vocation flows from the heart of God and blossoms in the good soil of faithful people, in the experience of fraternal love. Did not Jesus say: 'By this all men will know that you are my disciples, if you have love for one another' (*Jn* 13:35)? [. . .] The true joy of those who are called consists in believing and experiencing that he, the Lord, is faithful, and that with him we can walk, be disciples and witnesses of God's love, open our hearts to great ideals, to great things.

Message, 11 May 2014

————

Goodness is contagious

Saint Thomas said: '*bonum est diffusivum sui*' – the Latin is not very difficult! – good spreads. And joy also spreads. Do not be afraid to show the joy of having answered the Lord's call, of having responded to his choice of love and of bearing witness to his Gospel in service to the Church. And joy, true joy, is contagious; it is infectious . . . it impels one forward. Instead when you meet a seminarian who is excessively serious, too sad, or a novice like this, you think: but something has gone wrong here! The joy of the Lord is lacking, the joy that prompts you to serve, the joy of the encounter with Jesus which brings you to encounter others to proclaim Jesus. This is missing! There is no holiness in sadness, there isn't any! Saint Teresa – there are many Spaniards here and they know it well – said: 'a saint who is sad is a sad saint'. It is not worth much . . . When you see a seminarian, a priest, a sister or a novice with a long face, gloomy, who seems to have thrown a soaking wet blanket over their life, one of those heavy blankets . . . which pulls one down . . . Something has gone wrong! But please: never any sisters, never any priests with faces like 'chillies pickled in vinegar' – never!

Meeting, 6 July 2013

———

It's not enough to read the Gospel: you have to live it

The question we have to ask ourselves during this year is if and how we too are open to being challenged by the Gospel; whether the Gospel is truly the 'manual' for our daily living and the decisions we are called to make. The Gospel is demanding: it demands to be lived radically and sincerely. It is not enough to read it (even though the reading and study of Scripture is essential), nor is it enough to meditate on it (which we do joyfully each day). Jesus asks us to practise it, to put his words into effect in our lives.

Letter to all consecrated people, 21 November 2014

The true problem of the celibate is the lack of fertility

The joy that comes from Jesus. Think about this: when a priest – I say a priest, but also a seminarian – when a priest or a sister lacks joy he or she is sad; you might think: 'but this is a psychological problem'. No. It is true: that may be, that may be so, yes, it might. It might happen, some, poor things, fall sick . . . It might be so. However, in general it is not a psychological problem. Is it a problem of dissatisfaction? Well, yes! But what is at the heart of this lack of joy? It is a matter of celibacy. I will explain to you. You, seminarians, sisters, consecrate your love to Jesus, a great love. Your heart is for Jesus and this leads us to make the vow of chastity, the vow of celibacy. However, the vow of chastity and the vow of celibacy do not end at the moment the vow is taken, they endure . . . A journey that matures, that develops towards pastoral fatherhood, towards pastoral motherhood, and when a priest is not a father to his community, when a sister is not a mother to all those with whom she works, he or she becomes sad. This is the problem. For this reason I say to you: the root of sadness in pastoral life is precisely in the absence of fatherhood or motherhood that comes from living this consecration unsatisfactorily which on the contrary must lead us to fertility. It is impossible to imagine a priest or a sister who are not fertile: this is not Catholic! This is not Catholic! This is the beauty of consecration: it is joy, joy.

Meeting, 6 July 2013

The gift of a true priest

Priestly joy is a priceless treasure, not only for the priest himself but for the entire faithful people of God: that faithful people from which he is called to be anointed and which he, in turn, is sent to anoint.

Anointed with the oil of gladness so as to anoint others with the oil of gladness. Priestly joy has its source in the Father's love, and the Lord wishes the joy of this Love to be 'ours' and to be 'complete' (*Jn* 15:11). I like to reflect on joy by contemplating Our Lady, for Mary, the 'Mother of the living Gospel, is a wellspring of joy for God's little ones' (*Evangelii Gaudium*, 288). I do not think it is an exaggeration to say that the priest is very little indeed: the incomparable grandeur of the gift granted us for the ministry sets us among the least of men. The priest is the poorest of men unless Jesus enriches him by his poverty, the most useless of servants unless Jesus calls him his friend, the most ignorant of men unless Jesus patiently teaches him as he did Peter, the frailest of Christians unless the Good Shepherd strengthens him in the midst of the flock. No one is more 'little' than a priest left to his own devices; and so our prayer of protection against every snare of the Evil One is the prayer of our Mother: I am a priest because he has regarded my littleness (cf. *Lk* 1:48). And in that littleness we find our joy. Joy in our littleness!

Homily, 17 April 2014

The sense of being a priest lies outside of himself

Many people, in speaking of the crisis of priestly identity, fail to realize that identity presupposes belonging. The priest who tries to find his priestly identity by soul-searching and introspection may well encounter nothing more than 'exit' signs, signs that say: exit from yourself, exit to seek God in adoration, go out and give your people what was entrusted to you, for your people will make you feel and taste who you are, what your name is, what your identity is, and they will make you rejoice in that hundredfold which the Lord has promised to those who serve him. Unless you 'exit' from yourself, the oil grows rancid and the anointing cannot be fruitful. Going out from ourselves presupposes self-denial; it means poverty.

Homily, 17 April 2014

Live the present with passion

Living the present with passion means becoming 'experts in communion', 'witnesses and architects of the "plan for unity" which is the crowning point of human history in God's design'. In a polarized society, where different cultures experience difficulty in living alongside one another, where the powerless encounter oppression, where inequality abounds, we are called to offer a concrete model of community which, by acknowledging the dignity of each person and sharing our respective gifts, makes it possible to live as brothers and sisters.

So, be men and women of communion! Have the courage to be present in the midst of conflict and tension, as a credible sign of the presence of the Spirit who inspires in human hearts a passion for all to be one.

Letter to all consecrated people, 21 November 2014

———

Marked by the fire of passion for the kingdom

Humanity greatly needs to lay hold of the salvation brought by Christ. His disciples are those who allow themselves to be seized ever more by the love of Jesus and marked by the fire of passion for the kingdom of God and the proclamation of the joy of the Gospel. All the Lord's disciples are called to nurture the joy of evangelization. The bishops, as those primarily responsible for this proclamation, have the task of promoting the unity of the local Church in her missionary commitment. They are called to acknowledge that the joy of communicating Jesus Christ is expressed in a concern to proclaim him in the most distant places, as well as in a constant outreach to the peripheries of their own territory, where great numbers of the poor are waiting for this message.

Message, 8 June 2014

Sing the song of hope

To put ourselves with Jesus in the midst of his people. For this reason, we sense the challenge of finding and sharing a 'mystique' of living together, of mingling and encounter, of embracing and supporting one another, of stepping into this flood tide which, while chaotic, can [with the Lord] become a genuine experience of fraternity, a caravan of solidarity, a sacred pilgrimage . . . If we were able to take this route, it would be so good, so soothing, so liberating and hope-filled!

Homily, 2 February 2017

Where the consecrated are, there is joy

That the old saying will always be true: 'Where there are religious, there is joy'. We are called to know and show that God is able to fill our hearts to the brim with happiness; that we need not seek our happiness elsewhere; that the authentic fraternity found in our communities increases our joy; and that our total self-giving in service to the Church, to families and young people, to the elderly and the poor, brings us lifelong personal fulfilment.

Letter to all consecrated people, 21 November 2014

The joy of Jesus is our names written in heaven

The Evangelist tells us that the Lord sent the seventy-two disciples two by two into cities and villages to proclaim that the kingdom of God was near, and to prepare people to meet Jesus. After carrying out this mission of preaching, the disciples returned full of joy: joy is a dominant theme of this first and unforgettable missionary experience. Yet the divine Master told them: 'Do not rejoice because the demons are subject to you; but rejoice because your names are written in heaven. At that very moment Jesus rejoiced in the Holy Spirit and said: "I give you praise, Father . . ." And, turning to the disciples in private he said, "Blessed are the eyes that see what you see"' (*Lk* 10:20–21, 23).

Luke presents three scenes. Jesus speaks first to his disciples, then to the Father, and then again to the disciples. Jesus wanted to let the disciples share his joy, different and greater than anything they had previously experienced.

The disciples were *filled with joy*, excited about their power to set people free from demons. But Jesus cautioned them to rejoice not so much for the power they had received, but for the love they had received, 'because your names are written in heaven' (*Lk* 10:20). The disciples were given an experience of God's love, but also the possibility of sharing that love. And this experience is a cause for gratitude and joy in the heart of Jesus. Luke saw this jubilation in a perspective of the Trinitarian communion: 'Jesus rejoiced in the Holy Spirit', turning to the Father and praising him. This moment of deep joy springs from Jesus' immense filial love for his Father, Lord of heaven and earth, who hid these things from the wise and learned, and revealed them to the childlike (cf. *Lk* 10:21). God has both hidden and revealed, and in this prayer of praise it is his revealing that stands out. What is it that God has revealed and hidden? The mysteries of his kingdom, the manifestation of divine lordship in Jesus and the victory over Satan.

Message, 8 June 2014

———

The 'cities on the hill'

Monasteries, communities, centres of spirituality, schools, hospitals, family shelters – all these are places that the charity and creativity born of your charisms have brought into being, and with constant creativity must continue to bring into being. They should increasingly be the leaven for a society inspired by the Gospel, a 'city on a hill', which testifies to the truth and the power of Jesus' words.

Letter to all consecrated people, 21 November 2014

———

The call of God is always for our liberation and that of our brothers and sisters

To hear and answer the Lord's call is not a private and completely personal matter fraught with momentary emotion.

Rather, it is a specific, real and total commitment that embraces the whole of our existence and sets it at the service of the growth of God's kingdom on earth. The Christian vocation, rooted in the contemplation of the Father's heart, thus inspires us to solidarity in bringing liberation to our brothers and sisters, especially the poorest. A disciple of Jesus has a heart open to his unlimited horizons, and friendship with the Lord never means flight from this life or from the world. On the contrary, it involves a profound interplay between communion and mission.

Message, 29 March 2015

———

There is a lack of vocations where there is a lack of enthusiasm

Many parts of the world are experiencing a dearth of vocations to the priesthood and the consecrated life. Often this is due to the absence of contagious apostolic fervour in communities which lack enthusiasm and thus fail to attract. The joy of the Gospel is born of the encounter with Christ and from sharing with the poor. For this reason I encourage parish communities, associations and groups to live an intense fraternal life, grounded in love for Jesus and concern for the needs of the most disadvantaged. Wherever there is joy, enthusiasm and a desire to bring Christ to others, genuine vocations arise. Among these vocations, we should not overlook lay vocations to mission. There has been a growing awareness of the identity and mission of the lay faithful in the Church, as well as a recognition that they are called to take an increasingly important role in the spread of the Gospel. Consequently they need to be given a suitable training for the sake of an effective apostolic activity.

Message, 8 June 2014

————

Where there is brotherly love, God is calling

Today, too, Jesus lives and walks along the paths of ordinary life in order to draw near to everyone, beginning with the least, and to heal us of our infirmities and illnesses. I turn now to those who are well disposed to listen to the voice of Christ that rings out in the Church and to understand what their own vocation is. I invite you to listen to and follow Jesus, and to allow yourselves to be transformed within by his words, which 'are spirit and life' (*Jn* 6:62). Mary, the Mother of Jesus and ours, also says to us: 'Do whatever he tells you' (*Jn* 2:5). It will help you to participate in a communal journey that is able to release the best energies in you and around you. A vocation is a fruit that ripens in a well-cultivated field of mutual love that becomes mutual service, in the context of an authentic ecclesial life. No vocation is born of itself or lives for itself. A vocation flows from the heart of God and blossoms in the good soil of faithful people, in the experience of fraternal love. Did not Jesus say:

'By this all men will know that you are my disciples, if you have love for one another' (*Jn* 13:35)?

Message for the Day of Vocations, 11 May 2014

——————

Christ the Shepherd works in the priest

All who are called should know that genuine and complete joy does exist in this world: it is the joy of being taken from the people we love and then being sent back to them as dispensers of the gifts and counsels of Jesus, the one Good Shepherd who, with deep compassion for all the little ones and the outcasts of this earth, wearied and oppressed like sheep without a shepherd, wants to associate many others to his ministry, so as himself to remain with us and to work, in the person of his priests, for the good of his people.

Homily, 17 April 2014

——————

Remember your first love

I invite you to immerse yourself in the joy of the Gospel and nurture a love that can light up your vocation and your mission. I urge each of you to recall, as if you were making an interior pilgrimage, that 'first love' with which the Lord Jesus Christ warmed your heart, not for the sake of nostalgia but in order to persevere in joy. The Lord's disciples persevere in joy when they sense his presence, do his will and share with others their faith, hope and evangelical charity.

Message, 8 June 2014

THE GIFT AND EFFORT OF
BEING A WOMAN

'The Apostles and disciples
struggle to believe.
Women don't.'
3 April 2013

———

A Church without women?

A Church without women is like the college of the Apostles without Mary. The role of women in the Church is not simply that of maternity, being mothers, but much greater: it is precisely to be the icon of the Virgin, of Our Lady; what helps make the Church grow! But think about it, Our Lady is more important than the Apostles! She is more important! The Church is feminine. She is Church, she is bride, she is mother. But women, in the Church, must not only . . . I don't know how to say this in Italian . . . the role of women in the Church must not be limited to being mothers, workers, a limited role . . . No! It is something else!

Press conference, 28 July 2013

Sharing pastoral responsibilities

The Church acknowledges the indispensable contribution that women make to society through the sensitivity, intuition and other distinctive skill sets that they, more than men, tend to possess. I think, for example, of the special concern that women show to others, which finds a particular, even if not exclusive, expression in motherhood. I readily acknowledge that many women share pastoral responsibilities with priests, helping to guide people, families and groups and offering new contributions to theological reflection. But we need to create still broader opportunities for a more incisive female presence in the Church. Because 'the feminine genius is needed in all expressions in the life of society, the presence of women must also be guaranteed in the workplace' and in the various other settings where important decisions are made, both in the Church and in social structures.

Evangelii gaudium, 103

———

Woman is not fulfilled in servidumbre

I suffer – to tell you the truth – when I see in the Church or in Church organizations that the role of service, which we all have and should have . . . when a woman's role of service slides into *servidumbre* [servitude]. I don't know if that is how you say it in Italian. Do you understand me? Service. When I see women carrying out acts of servitude, it is because the role a woman should play is not properly understood. What presence do women have in the Church? Can it be developed further?

Address, 12 October 2013

———

A possible life, an incomparable contribution

Many women feel the need to be better recognized with respect to their rights, to the value of the tasks they normally carry out in the various sectors of social and professional life, and with respect to their aspirations within the family and within society. Some of them are weary and nearly crushed by the volume of duties and tasks, without sufficient help and understanding. Provision must be made to ensure that no woman, due to economic need, be forced into a job that is too hard, with hours that are overly burdensome, on top of adding to all her responsibilities as homemaker and educator of the children. But above all, it must be considered that the woman's commitments, on all levels of family life, also constitute an incomparable contribution to the life and future of society.

Message, 2 December 2014

———

Build reciprocity

Even though significant advances have been made in the recognition of women's rights and their participation in public life, in some countries much remains to be done to promote these rights. Unacceptable customs still need to be eliminated. I think particularly of the shameful ill-treatment to which women are sometimes subjected, domestic violence and various forms of enslavement which, rather than a show of masculine power, are craven acts of cowardice. The verbal, physical and sexual violence that women endure in some marriages contradicts the very nature of the conjugal union. I think of the reprehensible genital mutilation of women practised in some cultures, but also of their lack of equal access to dignified work and roles of decision-making. History is burdened by the excesses of patriarchal cultures that considered women inferior, yet in our own day, we cannot overlook the use of surrogate mothers and their exploitation, and those who believe that many of today's problems have arisen because of female emancipation. This argument, however, is not valid, 'it is false, untrue, a form of male chauvinism'. The equal dignity of men and women makes us rejoice to see old forms of discrimination disappear, and within families there is a growing reciprocity. If certain forms of feminism have arisen which we must consider inadequate, we must nonetheless see in the women's movement the working of the Spirit for a clearer recognition of the dignity and rights of women.

Amoris Laetitia, 54

Women, God entrusts you with the human being!

God entrusts man, the human being, in a special way to woman. What does this 'special entrusting', this special entrusting of the human being to woman mean? It seems evident to me that my Predecessor is referring to motherhood. Many things can change and have changed in cultural and social evolution, but the fact remains that it is woman who conceives, carries and delivers the children of men. And this is not merely a biological fact; it entails a wealth of implications both for woman herself, her way of being, and for her relationships, her relation to human life and to life in general. In calling woman to motherhood, God entrusted the human being to her in an entirely special way.

Address, 12 October 2015

Woman and man complement one another

Complementarity lies at the foundation of marriage and the family, which is the first school where we learn to appreciate our talents and those of others, and where we begin to acquire the art of living together. For most of us, the family is the principal place in which we begin to 'breathe' values and ideals, as we develop our full capacity for virtue and charity. At the same time, as we know, in families tensions arise: between egoism and altruism, between reason and passion, between immediate desires and long-term goals, and so on. But families also provide the environment in which these tensions are resolved: this is important. When we speak of complementarity between man and woman in this context, we must not confuse the term with the simplistic idea that all the roles and relationships of both sexes are confined to a single and static model. Complementarity assumes many forms, since every man and every woman brings their personal contribution – personal richness, their own charisma – to the marriage and to the upbringing of their children. Thus, complementarity becomes a great treasure. It is not only an asset but is also a thing of beauty.

Address, 17 November 2014

Two dangers that mortify woman's vocation

Here, however, two dangers are ever present, two opposite extremes that mortify woman and her vocation. The first is to reduce motherhood to a social role, to a task which, though regarded as noble in fact sets the woman and her potential aside and does not fully esteem her value in the structure of the community. This may happen both in civil and ecclesial circles. And, as a reaction to this, there is another danger in the opposite direction, that of promoting a kind of emancipation that, in order to fill areas that have been taken away from the male, abandons the feminine with all its precious attributes.

Address, 12 October 2013

The contribution of the feminine genius in the family, in society, in the Church

If in the world of work and in the public sphere a more incisive contribution of women's genius is important, this contribution remains essential within the family, which for we Christians is not simply a private place, but rather that 'domestic Church', whose health and prosperity is a condition for the health and prosperity of the Church and of society itself. Let us think of Our Lady: Our Lady creates something in the Church that priests, bishops and Popes cannot create. She is the authentic feminine genius. And let us think about Our Lady in families – about what Our Lady does in a family. It is clear that the presence of a woman in the domestic sphere is more necessary than ever, indeed for the transmission of sound moral principles and for the transmission of the faith itself to future generations.

Address, 25 January 2014

———

Learn from the women of the Resurrection to go out and share the faith!

The first witnesses of the Resurrection were the women. At dawn they went to the tomb to anoint Jesus' body and found the first sign: the empty tomb (cf. *Mk* 16:1). Their meeting with a messenger of God followed. He announced: 'Jesus of Nazareth, the Crucified One, has risen, he is not here'; (cf. vv. 5–6). The women were motivated by love and were able to accept this announcement with faith: they believed and passed it on straight away, they did not keep it to themselves but passed it on. They could not contain their joy in knowing that Jesus was alive, or the hope that filled their hearts. This should happen in our lives too. Let us feel the joy of being Christian! We believe in the Risen One who conquered evil and death! Let us have the courage to 'come out of ourselves' to take this joy and this light to all the places of our life! The Resurrection of Christ is our greatest certainty; he is our most precious treasure! How can we not share this treasure, this certainty with others? It is not only for us, it is to be passed on, to be shared with others.

General audience, 3 April 2013

―――――

The theological work of women reveals the unfathomable

I would like to invite you to reflect on the role that women can and should play in the field of theology. Indeed, 'the Church acknowledges the indispensable contribution which women make to society through the sensitivity, intuition and other distinctive skill sets which they, more than men, tend to possess. . . . I readily acknowledge that many women . . . [offer] new contributions to theological reflection' (*Evangelii gaudium*, 103). Thus, by virtue of their feminine genius, women theologians can detect, to the benefit of all, certain unexplored aspects of the unfathomable mystery of Christ, 'in whom are hid all the treasures of wisdom and knowledge'

(*Col* 2:3). I invite you to derive the greatest benefit of this specific contribution of women to the understanding of the faith.

Address, 5 December 2014

———

Keep on bearing witness!

This is part of the mission of women; of mothers, of women! Witnessing to their children, to their grandchildren, that Jesus is alive, is living, is risen. Mothers and women, carry on witnessing to this! It is the heart that counts for God, how open to him we are, whether we are like trusting children. However, this also makes us think about how women, in the Church and on the journey of faith, had and still have today a special role in opening the doors to the Lord, in following him and in communicating his Face, for the gaze of faith is always in need of the simple and profound gaze of love. The Apostles and disciples find it harder to believe. The women, not so. Peter runs to the tomb but stops at the empty tomb; Thomas has to touch the wounds on Jesus' body with his hands. On our way of faith it is also important to know and to feel that God loves us and not to be afraid to love him. Faith is professed with the lips and with the heart, with words and with love.

General audience, 3 April 2013

Risky choices, but choices made 'by women'

In the Church, this is how we should think of women: taking risky decisions, yet as women. This needs to be better explained. I believe that we have not yet come up with a profound theology of womanhood in the Church. All we say is: they can do this, they can do that, now they are altar servers, now they do the readings, they are in charge of Caritas [Catholic charity]. But there is more! We need to develop a profound theology of womanhood. That is what I think.

Press conference, 28 July 2013

————

You women are the conquerors of men

Woman possesses this great treasure of being able to give life, of being able to bestow tenderness, of being able to bestow peace and joy. There is only one model for you: Mary, the woman of fidelity, she who did not understand what was happening but who obeyed. She who, when she learned that her cousin was in need, went to her in haste, the Virgin of Readiness. She who fled like a refugee to that foreign land to save the life of her Son. She who helped her Son to grow and stayed with him, and when her Son began to preach, she followed him. She who endured all that was happening to that little child, to that growing youth. She who stayed by her

Son and told him what was the matter: 'Look, they have no wine'. She who, at the moment of the cross, was by him.

Video message, 26 April 2014

———

An icon of womanhood that should not be forgotten

On the cross, when Jesus endured in his own flesh the dramatic encounter of the sin of the world and God's mercy, he could feel at his feet the consoling presence of his mother and his friend. At that crucial moment, before fully accomplishing the work which his Father had entrusted to him, Jesus said to Mary: 'Woman, here is your son'. Then he said to his beloved friend: 'Here is your mother' (*Jn* 19:26–27). These words of the dying Jesus are not chiefly the expression of his devotion and concern for his mother; rather, they are a revelatory formula that manifests the mystery of a special saving mission. Jesus left us his mother to be our mother. Only after doing so did Jesus know that 'all was now finished' (*Jn* 19:28). At the foot of the cross, at the supreme hour of the new creation, Christ led us to Mary. He brought us to her because he did not want us to journey without a mother, and our people read in this maternal image all the mysteries of the Gospel. The Lord did not want to leave the Church without this icon of womanhood.

Evangelii gaudium, 285

No female machismo

It is necessary to broaden the opportunities for a stronger presence of women in the Church. I am wary of a solution that can be reduced to a kind of 'female *machismo*', because a woman has a different make-up than a man. But what I hear about the role of women is often inspired by an ideology of *machismo*. Women are asking deep questions that must be addressed. The Church cannot be herself without the woman and her role. The woman is essential for the Church. Mary, a woman, is more important than the bishops. I say this because we must not confuse the function with the dignity. We must therefore investigate further the role of women in the Church. We have to work harder to develop a profound theology of the woman. Only by making this step will it be possible to better reflect on their function within the Church. The feminine genius is needed wherever we make important decisions. The challenge today is this: to think about the specific place of women not least in those places where authority is exercised in various areas of the Church.

Interview with Father Antonio Spadaro, 19 August 2013

PART III

A HUNDREDFOLD
IN SUFFERING TOO

BEYOND TEARS AND LONELINESS

'If a person is scalded by milk,
he weeps when he sees the cow.'
9 January 2015

———

God joins in with our daily struggles

God himself is the one who takes the initiative and chooses to place himself, as he did with Mary, in our houses, in our daily struggles, filled with anxieties and also with desires. And it is precisely within our cities, our schools and universities, the squares and hospitals, that the most beautiful announcement we can hear is delivered: *'Rejoice, the Lord is with you.'* A joy that generates life, that generates hope, that makes itself flesh in the way we look at tomorrow, in the attitude with which we look at other people. A joy that becomes solidarity, hospitality, mercy towards everyone.

Homily, 25 March 2017

The Pope has his fears as well

Q. I have my fears; what are you afraid of?

A. (*Pope Francis*): Of myself! Fear ... Look, in the Gospel, Jesus says many times: 'Don't be afraid! Don't be afraid!' Many times, he says it. And why? Because he knows that fear is a normal thing, I would say. We are afraid of life, we are afraid of challenges, we are afraid of God ... We are all afraid, all of us. You mustn't worry about being afraid. You should feel this but not be afraid and then think: 'Why am I afraid?' And before God and before yourself try to sort out the situation or ask someone else to help. Fear is not a good counsellor, because it gives you poor advice. It sets you off on a path that is not the right one. That's why Jesus said so often: 'Don't be afraid! Don't be afraid!' We've also got to know ourselves, all of us: each of us must know himself and try to find the area in which we make the most mistakes, and be a bit afraid of that area. Because there is bad fear and good fear. Good fear is like caution. It is a cautious attitude: 'Look, you are weak at this, this and this, be cautious and don't fall. Bad fear is the one you say destroys you a little, wipes you out. It destroys you, it doesn't let you do something: this one is bad and you need to throw it out.

Interview with young people, 31 March 2014

The Gospel isn't make-up!

Jesus is Risen! We have seen him!

Let us allow this experience which is inscribed in the Gospel also to be imprinted in our hearts and shine forth from our lives. Let us allow the joyous wonder of Easter Sunday to shine forth in our thoughts, glances, behaviour, gestures and words . . . If only we were so luminous! But this is not just cosmetic! It comes from within, from a heart immersed in the source of this joy, like that of Mary Magdalene, who wept over the loss of her Lord and could hardly believe her eyes seeing him Risen.

Whoever experiences this becomes a witness of the Resurrection, for in a certain sense he himself has risen, she herself has risen. He or she is then capable of carrying a 'ray' of light of the Risen One into various situations: to those that are happy, making them more beautiful by preserving them from egoism; to those that are painful, bringing serenity and hope.

Regina coeli, 21 April 2014

———

When the devil comes masked as an angel

And here the first word that I wish to say to you: *joy*! Do not be men and women of sadness: a Christian can never be sad! Never give way to discouragement! Ours is not a joy born of having many possessions, but from having encountered a

Person: Jesus, in our midst; it is born from knowing that with him we are never alone, even at difficult moments, even when our life's journey comes up against problems and obstacles that seem insurmountable, and there are so many of them! And in this moment the enemy, the devil, comes, often disguised as an angel, and slyly speaks his word to us. Do not listen to him! Let us follow Jesus! We accompany, we follow Jesus, but above all we know that he accompanies us and carries us on his shoulders. This is our joy, this is the hope that we must bring to this world. Please do not let yourselves be robbed of hope! Do not let hope be stolen! The hope that Jesus gives us.

Homily, 24 March 2013

When we live between weeds and deserts

How often the seeds of goodness and hope that we try to sow seem to be choked by weeds of selfishness, hostility and injustice, not only all around us, but also in our own hearts. We are troubled by the growing gap in our societies between rich and poor. We see signs of an idolatry of wealth, power and pleasure which come at a high cost to human lives. Closer to home, so many of our own friends and contemporaries, even in the midst of immense material prosperity, are suffering from spiritual poverty, loneliness and quiet despair. God seems to be removed from the picture. It is almost as though a spiritual desert is beginning to spread throughout our world. It affects the young, too, robbing them of hope and even, in all too many cases, of life itself.

Address, 15 August 2014

———

Accept the challenge made to you by tears

Dear young men and women, our world today needs weeping. The marginalized weep, those who are neglected weep, the scorned weep, but those of us who have a relatively comfortable life, we don't know how to weep. Certain realities of life are seen only with eyes that are cleansed by tears. I ask each one of you to ask: Can I weep? Can I weep when I see a child who is hungry, on drugs and on the street, homeless, abandoned, mistreated or exploited as a slave by society? Or is my weeping the self-centred whining of those who weep because they want to have something else? This is the first thing I would like to say to you. Let's learn to weep. In the Gospel, Jesus wept. He wept for his dead friend. He wept in his heart for the family that lost its daughter. He wept in his heart when he saw the poor widowed mother who was burying her son. He was moved and he wept in his heart when he saw the crowds like sheep without a shepherd. If you don't learn how to weep, you are not a good Christian. And this is a challenge.

Address, 18 January 2015

The path of failure and the path of fulfilment

How much pain is caused in families because one of their members – often a young person – is in thrall to alcohol, drugs, gambling or pornography! How many people no longer see meaning in life or prospects for the future, how many have lost hope! And how many are plunged into this destitution by unjust social conditions, by unemployment, which takes away their dignity as breadwinners, and by lack of equal access to education and health care. In such cases, moral destitution can be considered impending suicide. This type of destitution, which also causes financial ruin, is invariably linked to the *spiritual destitution* that we experience when we turn away from God and reject his love. If we think we don't need God who reaches out to us through Christ, because we believe we can make do on our own, we are headed for a fall. God alone can truly save and free us.

Message for Lent, 2014

―――――

Don't risk pointless loneliness

The great danger in today's world, pervaded as it is by consumerism, is the desolation and anguish born of a complacent yet covetous heart, the feverish pursuit of frivolous pleasures, and a blunted conscience. Whenever our interior life becomes caught up in its own interests and concerns, there is no longer room for others, no place for the poor. God's voice is no longer heard, the quiet joy of his love is no longer felt, and the desire to do good fades. This is a very real danger for believers too. Many fall prey to it, and end up resentful, angry and listless. That is no way to live a dignified and fulfilled life; it is not God's will for us, nor is it the life in the Spirit which has its source in the heart of the risen Christ.

Evangelii gaudium, 2

The ultimate significance of your existence comes from God

The first kind of indifference in human society is indifference to God, which then leads to indifference to one's neighbour and to the environment. This is one of the grave consequences of a false humanism and practical materialism allied to relativism and nihilism. We have come to think that we are the source and creator of ourselves, our lives and society. We feel self-sufficient, prepared not only to find a substitute for God but to do completely without him. As a consequence, we feel that we owe nothing to anyone but ourselves, and we claim only rights.

Message for the World Day of Peace, 2016

What is my mind becoming?

As you continue along your path of teaching and learning in the university, try asking yourself: is my *forma mentis* becoming more individualistic or more solidary? If it is more solidary, it is a good sign because you will be going against the current, but going in the only direction that has a future and that offers a future. Solidarity, which is not proclaimed in words but rather experienced concretely, creates peace and hope for all countries and for the whole world.

Address, 17 February 2017

—————

Your Lents flow into Easter

There are Christians whose lives seem like Lent without Easter. I realize of course that joy is not expressed the same way at all times in life, especially at moments of great difficulty. Joy adapts and changes, but it always endures, even as a flicker of light born of our personal certainty that, when everything is said and done, we are infinitely loved. I understand the grief of people who have to endure great suffering, yet slowly but surely we all have to let the joy of faith slowly revive as a quiet yet firm trust, even amid the greatest distress.

Evangelii gaudium, 2

—————

God is not insensitive, Cain is: what about you?

Cain said he did not know what had happened to his brother, that he was not his brother's keeper. He did not feel responsible for his life, for his fate. He did not feel involved. He was indifferent to his brother, despite their common origin. How sad! What a sorry tale of brothers, of families, of human beings! This was the first display of indifference between brothers. God, however, is not indifferent. Abel's blood had immense value in his eyes, and he asked Cain to give an account of it. At the origin of the human race, God shows himself to be involved in mankind's destiny.

Message for the World Day of Peace, 2016

————

Are you living through the globalization of indifference?

God is not aloof from us. He is not aloof from us. Each one of us has a place in his heart. He knows us by name, he cares for us and he seeks us out whenever we turn away from him. He is interested in each of us; his love does not allow him to be indifferent to what happens to us. Usually, when we are healthy and comfortable, we forget about others (something God the Father never does): we are unconcerned with their problems, their sufferings and the injustices they endure . . . Our heart grows cold. As long as I am relatively healthy and comfortable, I don't think about those less well off. Today, this selfish attitude of indifference has taken on global pro-portions, to the extent that we can speak of a globalization of indifference. It is a problem which we, as Christians, need to confront.

Message for Lent, 2015

Avoid artificial paradises

In a culture often dominated by technology, sadness and loneliness appear to be on the rise, not least among young people. The future seems prey to an uncertainty that does not make for stability. This often gives rise to depression, sadness and boredom, which can gradually lead to despair. We need witnesses to hope and true joy if we are to dispel the illusions that promise quick and easy happiness through artificial paradises. The profound sense of emptiness felt by so many people can be overcome by the hope we bear in our hearts and by the joy that it gives. We need to acknowledge the joy that rises up in a heart touched by mercy. Let us keep in mind, then, the words of the Apostle: 'Rejoice in the Lord always' (*Phil* 4:4; cf. 1 *Thess* 5:16).

Misericordia et misera, 3

Don't be afraid of love

Youth is a time of life when your desire for a love which is genuine, beautiful and expansive begins to blossom in your hearts. How powerful is this ability to love and to be loved! Do not let this precious treasure be debased, destroyed or spoiled. That is what happens when we start to use our neighbours for our own selfish ends, even as objects of pleasure. Hearts are broken and sadness follows upon these negative experiences. I urge you: Do not be afraid of true love, the love that Jesus teaches us and which Saint Paul describes as 'patient and kind'. Paul says: 'Love is not jealous or boastful; it is not arrogant or rude. Love does not insist on its own way; it is not irritable or resentful; it does not rejoice at wrong, but rejoices in the right. Love bears all things, believes all things, hopes all things, endures all things' (1 Cor 13:4-8).

Message for World Youth Day, 31 January 2015

————

Gather the challenges against the dignity of the person

Being unemployed or not receiving a sufficiently large salary; not being able to have a home or a land in which to live; experiencing discrimination on account of one's faith, race or social status: these are just a few examples of many situations that attack the dignity of the person. In the face of such attacks, Christian mercy responds above all with vigilance and solidarity. How many situations exist today where we can restore dignity to individuals and make possible a truly humane life? Let us think only about the many children who suffer from forms of violence that rob them of the joy of life. I keep thinking of their sorrowful and bewildered faces. They are pleading for our help to be set free from the slavery of the contemporary world. These children are the young adults of tomorrow. How are we preparing them to live with dignity and responsibility? With what hope can they face their present or their future?

Misericordia et misera, 19

Live compassion, don't be discouraged

We always hear news of people who succumb to despair and do bad things . . . Despair leads them to many bad things. The reference is to one who is discouraged, who is weak, who feels discouraged by the burden of life and of his own faults, and no longer manages to pick himself up. In these cases, the closeness and warmth of the entire Church must be even more intense and loving, and must take on the exquisite form of compassion, which is not simply sympathy: compassion is to endure with the other, to suffer with the other, to draw near to the one who is suffering. A word, a caress, but given from the heart; this is compassion. For the one who needs comfort and consolation. This is more important than ever: Christian hope cannot do without genuine and concrete charity.

General audience, 8 February 2017

Be the eyes of the blind and the feet of the lame

Today too, how many Christians show, not by their words but by lives rooted in a genuine faith, that they are 'eyes to the blind' and 'feet to the lame'! They are close to the sick in need of constant care and help in washing, dressing and eating. This service, especially when it is protracted, can become tiring and burdensome. It is relatively easy to help someone for a few days but it is difficult to look after a person for months or even years, in some cases when he or she is no longer capable of expressing gratitude. And yet, what a great path of sanctification this is!

Message for the Day of the Sick, 2015

———

Ask for health, but also peace of mind

In Mary's concern we see reflected the tenderness of God. This same tenderness is present in the lives of all those persons who attend the sick and understand their needs, even the most imperceptible ones, because they look upon them with eyes full of love. How many times has a mother at the bedside of her sick child, or a child caring for an elderly parent, or a grandchild concerned for a grandparent, placed his or her prayer in the hands of Our Lady! For our loved ones who suffer because of illness we ask first for their health. Jesus himself showed the presence of the kingdom of God specifically through his healings: 'Go and tell John what you hear and see: the blind regain their sight, the lame walk, lepers are cleansed, the deaf hear, the dead are raised, and the poor have the good news proclaimed to them' (*Mt* 11:4–5). But love animated by faith makes us ask for them something greater than physical health: we ask for peace, a serenity in life that comes from the heart and is God's gift, the fruit of the Holy Spirit, a gift which the Father never denies to those who ask him for it with trust.

Message for the Day of the Sick, 2016

We like idols . . .

Faith means trusting in God – those who have faith trust in God – but there's a moment when, in meeting life's difficulties, man experiences the fragility of that trust and feels the need for various certainties – for tangible, concrete assurances. I entrust myself to God, but the situation is rather serious and I need a little more concrete reassurance. And there lies the danger! And then we are tempted to seek even ephemeral consolations that seem to fill the void of loneliness and alleviate the fatigue of believing. And we think we can find them in the security that money can give, in alliances with the powerful, in worldliness, in false ideologies. Sometimes we look for them in a god that can bend to our requests and magically intervene to change the situation and make it as we wish; an idol, indeed, that in itself can do nothing. It is impotent and deceptive. But we like idols; we love them!

General audience, 11 January 2017

———

Don't pursue the things that pass, or 'experimenting' with love

Some will say: joy is born from possessions, so they go in quest of the latest model of the smartphone, the fastest scooter, the showy car . . . but I tell you, it truly grieves me to see a priest or a sister with the latest model of a car: but this can't be! It can't be. You think: 'So do we now have to go by bicycle, Father?' Bicycles are good! Monsignor Alfred rides a bicycle. He goes by bike. I think that cars are necessary because there is so much work to be done, and also in order to get about . . . but choose a more humble car! And if you like the beautiful one, only think of all the children who are dying of hunger. That's all! Joy is not born from, does not come from, things we possess! Others say it comes from having the most extreme experiences or the thrill of the strongest sensations: young people like to walk on a knife edge, they really like it! Yet others like the trendiest clothes, entertainment in the most fashionable places – but I am not saying that sisters go to those places, I am saying it of young people in general. Yet others say joy comes from success with girls or with boys, and even from switching from one to another or from one to the other. This is insecurity in love, which is not certain: it is 'experimenting' with love. And we could go on . . . You too are in touch with this situation which you cannot ignore.

Meeting with seminarians and novices, 6 July 2013

Let the water of your life become precious wine

We too, whether healthy or sick, can offer up our toil and sufferings like the water that filled the jars at the wedding feast of Cana and was turned into the finest wine. By quietly helping those who suffer, as in illness itself, we take our daily cross upon our shoulders and follow the Master (cf. *Lk* 9:23).

Even though the experience of suffering will always remain a mystery, Jesus helps us to reveal its meaning.

If we can learn to obey the words of Mary, who says: 'Do whatever he tells you', Jesus will always change the water of our lives into precious wine.

Message for the Day of the Sick, 2016

———

The doors of consolation

If we want to experience his consolation, we must give way to the Lord in our lives. And in order for the Lord to abide continually in us, we must open the doors of our hearts to him and not keep him outside. There are *doors of consolation* that must always be open, because Jesus especially loves to enter through them: the Gospel we read every day and carry around with us, our silent prayer in adoration, Confession, the Eucharist. It is through these doors that the Lord enters and gives new flavour to reality. When the door of our heart is closed, however, his light cannot enter in and everything remains dark. We then get accustomed to pessimism, to things which aren't right, to realities that never change. We end up absorbed in our own sadness, in the depths of anguish, isolated. If, on the other hand, we open wide the doors of consolation, the light of the Lord enters in!

Homily, 1 October 2016

Nourish the roots of your hope

Hope is a gift of God. We must ask for it. It is placed deep within each human heart in order to shed light on this life, so often troubled and clouded by so many situations that bring sadness and pain. We need to nourish the roots of our hope so that they can bear fruit; primarily, the certainty of God's closeness and compassion, despite whatever evil we have done. There is no corner of our heart that cannot be touched by God's love. Whenever someone makes a mistake, the Father's mercy is all the more present, awakening repentance, forgiveness, reconciliation and peace.

Homily, 6 November 2016

———

Are you suffering? Get to know God 'not by hearsay'!

Even when illness, loneliness and inability make it hard for us to reach out to others, the experience of suffering can become a privileged means of transmitting grace and a source for gaining and growing in *sapientia cordis*. We come to understand how Job, at the end of his experience, could say to God: 'I had heard of you by the hearing of the ear, but now my eye sees you' (*Job* 42:5). People immersed in the mystery of suffering and pain, when they accept these in faith, can themselves become living witnesses of a faith capable of embracing suffering, even without being able to understand its full meaning.

Message for the Day of the Sick, 2015

Lights that dazzle and lights that illuminate

In our life too, there are several stars, lights that twinkle and guide. It is up to us to choose which ones to follow. For example, there are *flashing lights* that come and go, like the small pleasures of life: though they may be good, they are not enough, because they do not last long and they do not leave the peace we seek. Then there is the *dazzling limelight* of money and success, which promises everything, and at once. It is seductive, but with its intensity, blinds and causes dreams of glory to fade into the thickest darkness. The Magi, instead, invite us to follow a *steady light*, a *gentle light* that does not wane, because it is not of this world: it comes from heaven and shines . . . where? In the heart.

This true light is the light of the Lord, or rather, *it is the Lord himself*. He is our light: a light that does not dazzle, but accompanies and bestows a unique joy.

Angelus, 6 January 2017

———

If you only share the crumbs you don't take away the hunger

It is simple to give a part of the profits, without embracing and touching the people who receive those 'crumbs'. Instead, just five loaves and two fishes can feed the multitude if they are the sharing of all our life. In the logic of the Gospel, if one does not give all of himself, he never gives enough of himself.

Address, 4 February 2017

No wise person is closed up in themselves

Wisdom of the heart means going forth from ourselves towards our brothers and sisters. Occasionally our world forgets the special value of time spent at the bedside of the sick, since we are in such a rush; caught up as we are in a frenzy of doing, of producing, we forget about giving ourselves freely, taking care of others, being responsible for others. Behind this attitude there is often a lukewarm faith that has forgotten the Lord's words: 'You did it unto me' (*Mt* 25:40).

Message for the Day of the Sick, 2015

———

Do you want to be like God or like the idols 'that do not speak'?

Psalm 115 is recited as follows:

'Their idols are silver and gold
    the work of men's hands.
They have mouths, but do not speak;
    eyes, but do not see.
They have ears, but do not hear;
    noses, but do not smell.
They have hands, but do not feel;
    feet, but do not walk;
    and they do not make a sound in their throat.
Those who make them are like them;
    so are all who trust in them!' (vv. 4–8)

The psalmist also presents to us, a bit ironically, the absolutely ephemeral character of these idols. And we must understand that these are not merely figures made of metal or other materials but are also those we build in our minds: when we trust in limited realities that we transform into absolute values, or when we diminish God to fit our own template and our ideas of divinity; a god that looks like us is understandable, predictable, just like the idols mentioned in the Psalm. Man, the image of God, manufactures a god in his own image, and it is also a poorly realized image. It does not hear, does not act, and above all, it cannot speak. But we are happier to turn to idols than to turn to the Lord. Many times, we are happier with the ephemeral hope that this false idol gives us, than with the great and sure hope that the Lord gives us.

The message of the Psalm is very clear: if you place hope in idols, you become like them: hollow images with hands that do not feel, feet that do not walk, mouths that cannot speak. You no longer have anything to say; you become unable to help, to change things, unable to smile, to give of yourself, incapable of love. And we, men of the Church, run this risk when we 'are made worldly'. We need to abide in the world but defend ourselves from the world's illusions, which are these idols that I mentioned.

General audience, 11 January 2017

Our obsessions

We distance ourselves from God's love when we search incessantly for earthly goods and riches, thus showing an exaggerated liking for these realities.

Jesus tells us that this frantic search is illusory and a cause of unhappiness. He gives his disciples a fundamental rule of life: 'seek first and foremost the kingdom of God' (cf. *Mt* 6:33). It is a matter of fulfilling the plan that Jesus proclaimed in the *sermon on the mount*, entrusting oneself to God who does not disappoint – many friends, or many people whom we believed were friends, have disappointed us; God never disappoints! – dedicating oneself as faithful stewards of the goods that he has given us, even the earthly goods, but without 'overdoing things' as if everything, even our salvation, depended only on us. This evangelical attitude requires a clear choice, which today's reading indicates precisely: 'You cannot serve God and mammon' (*Mt* 6:24). Either the Lord, or fascinating but illusory idols. This choice that we are called to make then has an impact on many of our actions, plans and commitments. It means choosing to act very clearly and to continually renew, because the temptation to reduce everything to money, pleasure and power is relentless. There are so many such temptations.

Angelus, 26 February 2017

What's more important, you or your beauty?

In contrast to hoping in a Lord of life who, through his Word created the world and leads our existence, we turn to dumb effigies. Ideologies with their claim to the absolute, wealth – and this is a great idol – power and success, vanity, with their illusion of eternity and omnipotence, values such as physical beauty and health: when they become idols to which everything is sacrificed, they are all things that confuse the mind and the heart, and instead of supporting life, they lead to death. It is terrible to hear, and painful to the soul: something that once, years ago, I heard in the Diocese of Buenos Aires: a good woman – very beautiful – boasted about her beauty. She said, as if it were natural: 'Yes, I had to have an abortion because my figure is very important'. These are idols, and they lead you down the wrong path, and do not give you happiness.

General audience, 11 January 2017

––––––

Don't trust in the certainty given to you by fortune tellers

Once, in Buenos Aires, I had to go from one church to another, a thousand metres, more or less. And I did so on foot. And between them there is a park, and in the park there were little tables, where many, many fortune tellers were sitting. It was full of people who were even waiting in line. You would give them your hand and they'd begin, but the conversation was always the same: 'There is a woman in your life, there is a darkness that comes, but everything will be fine . . .' And then, you paid. And this gives you security? It is the security of – allow me to use the word – nonsense. Going to a seer or to a fortune teller who reads cards: this is an idol! This is the idol, and when we are so attached to them, we buy false hope.

General audience, 11 January 2017

————

The corrupt are not happy today, and won't be in the future

I am thinking, for example, of people who have responsibility for others and allow themselves to become corrupt; do you think a corrupt person will be happy on the other side? No, all the fruit of his corruption has corrupted his heart and it will be difficult for him to go to the Lord. I am thinking of those who live off human trafficking or slave labour; do you think these people who traffic persons, who exploit people through slave labour have love for God in their hearts? No, they haven't fear of the Lord and they are not happy. They are not. I am thinking of those who manufacture weapons for fomenting wars; just think about what kind of job this is. I am certain that if I were to ask: how many of you manufacture weapons? No one, no one. These weapons manufacturers don't come to hear the Word of God! These people manufacture death, they are merchants of death and they make death into a piece of merchandise. May fear of the

Lord make them understand that one day all things will come to an end and they will have to give account to God.

General audience, 11 June 2014

———

He knows better than we do . . .

We ask the Lord for life, for health, for love, for happiness; and it is right to do so, but with the understanding that God is able to bring life even from death, that we can experience peace even in sickness, and that there can be calm even in loneliness, and happiness even in tears. It is not for us to instruct God about what he must do, about what we need. He knows better than we do, and we must have faith, because his ways and his thoughts are different from ours.

General audience, 25 January 2017

———

The mother dough and the mouldy Gospel

When there were no refrigerators, to preserve the *mother dough* of the bread, they gave a small amount of their own leavened dough to a neighbour, and when they needed to make bread again they received a handful of leavened dough from that woman or from another who had received it in her turn. It is reciprocity. Communion is not only the *sharing* but also the *multiplying* of goods, the creation of new bread, of new goods, of new Good with a capital 'G'. The living principle of the Gospel remains active only if we give it, because it is love, and love is active when we love, not when we read novels or when we watch soap operas. If instead we possessively keep it all and only for ourselves, it goes mouldy and dies. The Gospel can grow mouldy. The economy of communion will have a future if you give it to everyone and it does not remain only inside your 'house'. Give it to everyone, firstly to the poor and the young, who are those who need it most and know how to make the gift received bear fruit! To have life in abundance one must learn to give: not only the profits of businesses, but of yourselves. The first gift of the entrepreneur is of his or her own person: your money, although important, is too little.

Address, 4 February 2017

————

Be missionaries of joy even in times of difficulty

Saint Paul again indicates the conditions for being 'missionaries of joy': praying constantly, always giving thanks to God, giving way to his Spirit, seeking the good and avoiding evil (cf. *1 Thess* 5:17–22). If this becomes our lifestyle, then the Good News will be able to enter so many homes and help people and families to rediscover that in Jesus lies salvation. In him it is possible to find inner peace and the strength to face different life situations every day, even the heaviest and most difficult. No one has ever heard of a sad saint with a mournful face. This is unheard of! It would be a contradiction. The Christian's heart is filled with peace because he knows how to place his joy in the Lord even when going through the difficult moments in life. To have faith does not mean to never have difficult moments but to have the strength to face those moments knowing that we are not alone. And this is the peace that God gives to his children.

Angelus, 14 December 2014

FROM ERRORS TO FORGIVENESS

'It's a good thing to have dialogue with your own mistakes,
because they follow you.'

31 March 2014

How do you want to be saved?

How do I want to be saved? My way? According to a
spirituality that is good, that is good for me, but that is set,
having everything defined and no risks? Or in a divine
manner, that is, on the path of Jesus, who always surprises
us, who always opens the doors for us to that mystery of
the almighty power of God, which is mercy and forgiveness?

Homily at Domus Sanctae Marthae, 3 October 2014

I learn from my mistakes

I have made mistakes, I make mistakes. In the Bible, in the
Book of Wisdom, it says that the most righteous of men makes

seven mistakes a day! Meaning that we all make mistakes. They say that man is the only animal who falls twice on the same spot because he does not immediately learn from his mistakes. You might say, 'I haven't made any mistakes', but it doesn't make things better. This takes you to vanity, to pride . . . I think that the mistakes even in my life have been, and are, great teachers in life. Great teachers: they teach you so much. They humiliate you too, because you can feel like a superman, a superwoman, and then you make a mistake, and this humiliates you and puts you in your place. I wouldn't say that I've learned from all my mistakes: no, I think I didn't learn from some of them because I'm stubborn, and it isn't easy to learn. But I have learned from many mistakes, and that did me good, it did me good. And it's also important to acknowledge your mistakes: I made this mistake, I made a mistake here, a mistake there . . . And also be careful not to return to the same mistake, draw water from the same well.

Interview with young people, 31 March 2014

Jesus forgives with a caress

God doesn't forgive with a decree but with a caress. Jesus goes beyond the law and forgives us by caressing the wounds of our sins. How many of us deserve condemnation! And it would also be just. But he forgives! How? With this mercy that does not wipe out sin: it is God's forgiveness that erases it, while mercy goes beyond.

Like the sky: we look at the sky, so many stars, but when the sun rises in the morning, with so much light, you can't see the stars. God's mercy is like that: a great light of love, of tenderness.

God forgives not with a decree but with a caress, caressing the wounds of our sins because he is involved in the forgiveness, he is involved in our salvation.

Jesus takes Confession. He does not humiliate the woman taken in adultery, he doesn't say to her: what did you do, when did you do it, how did you do it and who did you do it with? He tells her to go and not sin again: God's mercy is great, Jesus' mercy is great: forgiving us by caressing us.

Homily at Domus Sanctae Marthae, 7 April 2014

———

Faith doesn't make evil go away, but it offers a key for goodness

Illness, above all grave illness, always places human existence in crisis and brings with it questions that dig deep. Our first response may at times be one of rebellion: why has this happened to me? We can feel desperate, thinking that all is lost, that things no longer have meaning . . .

In these situations, faith in God is on the one hand tested, yet at the same time can reveal all of its positive resources. Not because faith makes illness, pain, or the questions which they raise, disappear, but because it offers a key by which we can discover the deepest meaning of what we are experiencing; a key that helps us to see how illness can be the way to draw nearer to Jesus who walks at our side, weighed down by the cross.

Message for the Day of the Sick, 2016

Joy for the adulteress and the sinner

What great joy welled up in the heart of these two women: the adulteress and the sinner! Forgiveness made them feel free at last and happy as never before. Their tears of shame and pain turned into the smile of a person who knows that he or she is loved. Mercy gives rise to *joy*, because our hearts are opened to the hope of a new life. The joy of forgiveness is inexpressible, yet it radiates all around us whenever we experience forgiveness. Its source is in the love with which God comes to meet us, breaking through walls of selfishness that surround us, in order to make us in turn instruments of mercy.

Misericordia et misera, 3

Arise, shine!

So said Isaiah, prophesying this joy of today in Jerusalem, 'Arise, shine'. At the beginning of each day we can welcome this invitation: *arise, shine*, and follow today – among the many shooting stars in the world – the bright star of Jesus! Following it, we will experience the joy, as happened to the

Magi, who 'when they saw the star, they rejoiced exceedingly with great joy' (Mt 2:10); because *where there is God, there is joy*. Those who have encountered Jesus have experienced the miracle of light that pierces the darkness and know this light that illuminates and brightens. I would like, with great respect, to invite everyone not to fear this light and to open up to the Lord. Above all, I would like to say to those who have lost the strength to seek, who are tired, to those who, overwhelmed by the darkness of life, have extinguished this yearning: arise, take heart, the light of Jesus can overcome the deepest darkness. Arise, take heart!

Angelus, 6 January 2017

Better red than yellow

And we must never tire of going to ask for forgiveness. You may feel ashamed to tell your sins, but as our mothers and our grandmothers used to say, it is better to be red once than yellow a thousand times. We blush once but then our sins are forgiven and we go forward.

General audience, 20 November 2013

When does Jesus weep?

When Jesus sees this tragedy of resistance, and also when he sees ours, he weeps. He wept in front of Lazarus' tomb; he cried looking at Jerusalem as he said, 'You who kill the prophets and stone all those who are sent to you, how often would I have gathered your children together as a hen gathers her brood under her wings!' And he also weeps facing this tragedy of not accepting his salvation as the Father wants it.

Homily at Domus Sanctae Marthae, 3 October 2014

We have all made mistakes, we can change

We can all make mistakes: all of us. And in one way or another we have made mistakes. Hypocrisy leads us to overlook the possibility that people can change their lives; we put little trust in rehabilitation, rehabilitation into society. But in this way we forget that we are all sinners and often, without being aware of it, we too are prisoners. At times we are locked up within our own prejudices or enslaved to the idols of a false sense of wellbeing. At times we get stuck in our own ideologies or absolutize the laws of the market even as they crush other people. At such times, we imprison ourselves behind the walls of individualism and self-sufficiency, deprived of the truth that sets us free. Pointing the finger at someone who has made mistakes cannot become an alibi for concealing our own contradictions.

We know that in God's eyes no one can consider himself just (cf. *Rom* 2:1–11). But no one can live without the certainty of finding forgiveness!

Homily, 6 November 2016

Don't walk in the darkness of one who lies to himself

What does it mean to walk in darkness? Because in the dark-ness of our lives we also have moments when everything, even in our own conscience, is dark. Walking in darkness means being satisfied with oneself. Being convinced that one doesn't need salvation. That is the darkness! And when you walk along that path of darkness, it isn't easy to turn back. That is why John (cf. 1 *Jn* 1, 5–2, 2) goes on, perhaps this way of thinking makes him think: 'If we say we are without sin, we deceive ourselves and the truth is not in us'. Take care of your sins, of our sins: we are all sinners, all of us. That is our starting point.

But if we confess our sins he is faithful and just enough to forgive our sins and cleanse us of all iniquity . . . When the Lord forgives us he makes justice. Yes, he makes justice first to himself, because he came to save and when he forgives us he makes justice to himself. 'I am your saviour' and he wel-comes us . . .

'As a father has compassion on his children, so the Lord has compassion on those who fear him. (cf. *Psalm* 102), towards those who walk away from him, the compassion of the Lord. He always understands us, but he does not let us speak: he knows everything. 'Be calm, go in peace', that peace that he alone gives.

Homily at Domus Sanctae Marthae, 29 April 2013

The true battlefield is your heart

Jesus himself lived in violent times. Yet he taught that the true battlefield, where violence and peace meet, is the human heart: for 'it is from within, from the human heart, that evil intentions come' (*Mk* 7:21). But Christ's message in this regard offers a radically positive approach. He unfailingly preached God's unconditional love, which welcomes and forgives. He taught his disciples to love their enemies (cf. *Mt* 5:44) and to turn the other cheek (cf. *Mt* 5:39). When he stopped her accusers from stoning the woman caught in adultery (cf. *Jn* 8:1–11), and when, on the night before he died, he told Peter to put away his sword (cf. *Mt* 26:52), Jesus marked out the path of non-violence. He walked that path to the very end, to the cross, whereby he became our peace and put an end to hostility (cf. *Eph* 2:14–16). Whoever accepts the Good News of Jesus is able to acknowledge the violence within and be healed by God's mercy, becoming in turn an instrument of reconciliation. In the words of Saint Francis of Assisi: 'As you announce peace with your mouth, make sure that you have greater peace in your hearts'.

Message for the World Day of Peace, 2017

Standing water is the first to go bad

We all know that when water stands still it stagnates. There's a saying in Spanish that says: 'Standing water is the first to go bad'. Do not stand still. We all have to walk, to take a step every day, with the Lord's help. God is Father, he is mercy, he always loves us. If we seek him, he welcomes us and forgives us. As I said, he never tires of forgiving. This is the motto of this visit: 'God doesn't tire of forgiving'. He makes us rise and fully restores our dignity. God has a memory, he is not forgetful. God does not forget us, he always remembers. There is a passage in the Bible, from the prophet Isaiah, which says: 'Even should a mother forget her child – which is impossible – I will never forget you' (cf. *Is* 49:15). And this is true: God thinks about me, God remembers me. I am in God's memory.

Address, 5 July 2014

————

The unhappiness of the vengeful

If we live according to the law 'an eye for an eye, a tooth for a tooth', we will never escape from the spiral of evil. The evil one is clever, and deludes us into thinking that with our human justice we can save ourselves and save the world! In reality, only the justice of God can save us! And the justice of God is revealed in the cross: the cross is the judgement of God on us all and on this world. But how does God judge us? By giving his life for us! Here is the supreme act of justice that defeated the prince of this world once and for all; and this supreme act of justice is the supreme act of mercy. Jesus calls us all to follow this path: Be merciful, even as your

Father is merciful (*Lk* 6:36). I now ask of you one thing. In silence, let's all think . . . everyone think of a person with whom we are annoyed, with whom we are angry, someone we do not like. Let us think of that person and in silence, at this moment, let us pray for this person and let us become merciful with this person.

Angelus, 15 September 2013

The enemy is also a human being

'Love your enemies and pray for those who persecute you' (*Mt.* 6: 44). And this is not easy. These words should not be seen as an approval of evil carried out by an enemy, but as an invitation to a loftier perspective, a magnanimous perspective, similar to that of the heavenly Father, who, Jesus says, 'makes his sun rise on the evil and on the good, and sends rain on the just and on the unjust' (v. 45). An enemy, in fact, is also a human being, created as such in God's image, despite the fact that in the present, that image may be tarnished by shameful behaviour.

When we speak of 'enemies', we should not think about people who are different or far removed from us; let us also talk about ourselves, as we may come into conflict with our neighbour, at times with our relatives. How many hostilities exist within families – how many! Let us think about this. Enemies are also those who speak ill of us, who defame us and do us harm. It is not easy to digest this. We are called to respond to each of them with good, which also has strategies inspired by love.

Angelus, 19 February 2017

———

Take heart, pass through his narrow door!

Take heart, have the courage to enter through his door. Everyone is invited to cross the threshold of this door, to cross the threshold of faith, to enter into his life and to make him enter our life, so that he may transform it, renew it and give it full and enduring joy.

In our day we pass in front of so many doors that invite us to come in, promising a happiness that later we realize lasts only an instant, exhausts itself with no future. But I ask you: by which door do we want to enter? And who do we want to let in through the door of our life? I would like to say forcefully: let's not be afraid to cross the threshold of faith in Jesus, to let him enter our life more and more, to step out of our selfishness, our closure, our indifference to others so that Jesus may illuminate our life with a light that never goes out. It is not a firework, not a flash of light! No, it is a peaceful light that lasts forever and gives us peace. Consequently it is the light we encounter if we enter through Jesus' door.

Of course Jesus' door is a narrow one, but not because it is a torture chamber. No, not for that reason! Rather, because he asks us to open our hearts to him, to recognize that we are sinners in need of his salvation, his forgiveness and his love in order to have the humility to accept his mercy and to let ourselves be renewed by him.

Angelus, 25 August 2013

———

Don't reproach others, show them the better way

Sometimes we try to correct or convert a sinner by scolding him, by pointing out his mistakes and wrongful behaviour. Jesus' attitude toward Zacchaeus shows us another way: that of showing those who err their value, the value that God continues to see in spite of everything, despite all their mistakes. This may bring about a positive surprise, which softens the heart and spurs the person to bring out the good that he has within himself. It gives people the confidence that makes them grow and change. This is how God acts with all of us: he is not blocked by our sin, but overcomes it with love and makes us feel nostalgia for the good. We have all felt this nostalgia for the good after a mistake. And this is what God Our Father does, this is what Jesus does. There is no one who does not have some good quality. And God looks at it to draw that person away from evil.

Angelus, 30 October 2016

———

Each of us carries the richness and burdens of our personal history

We must remember that each of us carries the richness and the burdens of our personal history; this is what makes us different from everyone else. Our life, with its joys and sorrows, is something unique and unrepeatable that takes place under the merciful gaze of God. This demands, especially of priests, a careful, profound and farsighted spiritual discernment, so that everyone, none excluded, no matter the situation a person is living in, can feel accepted by God, participate actively in the life of the community and be part of that People of God which journeys tirelessly towards the fullness of his kingdom of justice, love, forgiveness and mercy.

Misericordia et misera, 14

―――――

How do you see the path of your salvation?

Which do I think is the path of my salvation: the path of Jesus, or a different one? Am I free to accept salvation, or am I confusing freedom with autonomy and I want my salvation, the one I think is the right one? Do I think that Jesus is the teacher who instructs us in salvation or do I go all over the place hiring gurus to each me a different one? Do I seek a more reliable path, or take refuge under the roof of the prescriptions and the many man-made commandments? So do I feel safe, and with this safety – and it's a bit hard to say this – am I buying my salvation that Jesus gives gratuitously, with the gratuitousness of God?

Homily at the Chapel of Domus Sanctae Marthae, 3 October 2014

Be courageous, go to Confession!

Shame is also good, it is healthy to feel a little shame, because being ashamed is salutary. In my country, when a person feels no shame, we say that he is 'shameless', a '*sinvergüenza*'. But shame too does good, because it makes us more humble, and the priest receives this Confession with love and tenderness and forgives us on God's behalf. Also from a human point of view, in order to unburden oneself, it is good to talk with a brother and tell the priest these things that are weighing so much on my heart. And one feels that one is unburdening oneself before God, with the Church, with his brother. Do not be afraid of Confession! When one is in line to go to Confession, one feels all these things, even shame, but then when one finishes Confession one leaves free, grand, beautiful, forgiven, candid, happy. This is the beauty of Confession! I would like to ask you – but don't say it aloud, everyone respond in his heart: when was the last time you made your Confession? Everyone think about it . . . Two days, two weeks, two years, twenty years, forty years? Everyone counts, everyone says 'When was the last time I went to Confession?' And if much time has passed, do not lose another day. Go, the priest will be good. Jesus is there, and Jesus is more benevolent than priests, Jesus receives you, he receives you with so much love. Be courageous and go to Confession!

General audience, 19 February 2014

The flock and the wolf

Jesus comes forth from an unjust trial, from a cruel interrogation and he looks in the eyes of Peter, and Peter weeps. We ask that he look at us and that we allow ourselves to be looked upon and to weep and that he give us the grace to be ashamed, so that, like Peter, forty days later, we can reply: 'You know that I love you'; and hear him say: 'go back and feed my sheep' – and I would add – 'let no wolf enter the sheepfold'.

Homily at the Chapel of Domus Sanctae Marthae, 7 July 2014

A HUNDREDFOLD AND ETERNITY

'The Christian never loses peace,
when he is a true Christian.'
14 December 2014

———

I'm afraid of seeing it approaching

Each time we face our death or that of a person dear to us, we feel that our faith is put to the test. All our doubts emerge, all our frailty, and we ask ourselves: 'But will there truly be life after death . . .? Will I still be able to see and embrace again the people I have loved . . .?' A woman asked me this question several days ago in an audience, revealing doubt: 'Will I meet my loved ones?' In the current context, we too need to return to the root and foundation of our faith, so as to become aware of how much God did for us in Jesus Christ and what our death means. We are all a little frightened due to this uncertainty about death. It reminds me of an elderly man, a kind old man, who said: 'I am not afraid of death. I am a bit afraid of seeing it approaching'. He was afraid of this.

General audience, 1 February 2017

———

We are heirs to great dreams

Simeon's canticle is the hymn of the believer, who at the end of his days can exclaim: 'It is true, hope in God never disappoints' (cf. *Rm* 5:5). God never deceives us. Simeon and Anna, in their old age, were capable of a new fruitfulness, and they testify to this in song. Life is worth living in hope, because the Lord keeps his promise. Jesus himself will later explain this promise in the synagogue of Nazareth: the sick, prisoners, those who are alone, the poor, the elderly and sinners, all are invited to take up this same hymn of hope. Jesus is with them, Jesus is with us (cf. *Lk* 4:18–19).

We have inherited this hymn of hope from our elders. They made us part of this process. In their faces, in their lives, in their daily sacrifice we were able to see how this praise was embodied. We are heirs to the dreams of our elders, heirs to the hope that did not disappoint our founding mothers and fathers, our older brothers and sisters. We are heirs to those who have gone before us and had the courage to dream. Like them, we too want to sing, 'God does not deceive; hope in him does not disappoint'. God comes to meet his people.

Homily, 2 February 2017

The challenge of the final passage

The moment of death. The Church has always experienced this dramatic passage in the light of Christ's Resurrection, which opened the way to the certainty of the life to come. We have a great challenge to face, especially in contemporary culture, which often tends to trivialize death to the point of treating it as an illusion or hiding it from sight. Yet death must be faced and prepared for as a painful and inescapable passage, yet one charged with immense meaning, for it is the ultimate act of love towards those we leave behind and towards God whom we go forth to meet. In all religions, the moment of death, like that of birth, is accompanied by a religious presence. As Christians, we celebrate the funeral liturgy as a hope-filled prayer for the soul of the deceased and for the consolation of those who suffer the loss of their loved one.

Misericordia et misera, 15

――――――

We will all have a sunrise. What will yours be like?

Hope is a little like leaven that expands our souls. There are difficult moments in life, but with hope the soul goes forward and looks ahead to what awaits us. Today is a day of hope. Our brothers and sisters are in the presence of God and we shall also be there, through the pure grace of the Lord, if we walk along the way of Jesus. The Apostle John concludes: 'every one who thus hopes in him purifies himself as he is pure' (v. 3). Hope also purifies us, it lightens us; this purification in hope in Jesus Christ makes us go in haste, readily. Today before evening falls each one of us can think of the twilight of life: 'What will my passing away be like?' All of us will experience sunset, all of us! Do we look at it with hope? Do we look with that joy at being welcomed by the Lord? This is a Christian thought that gives us hope. Today is a day of joy; however it is serene and tranquil joy, a peaceful joy. Let us think about the passing away of so many of our brothers and sisters who have preceded us, let us think about the evening of our life, when it will come. And let us think about our hearts and ask ourselves: 'Where is my heart anchored?' If it is not firmly anchored, let us anchor it beyond, on that shore, knowing that hope does not disappoint because the Lord Jesus does not disappoint.

Homily, 1 November 2013

Watch out! You won't be able to take power or pride into eternity

When a person lives in evil, when one blasphemes against God, when one exploits others, when he tyrannizes them, when he lives only for money, for vanity, or power, or pride, then the holy fear of God sends us a warning: be careful! With all this power, with all this money, with all of your pride, with all your vanity, you will not be happy. No one can take it with them to the other side: not the money, power, vanity or pride. Nothing! We can only take the love that God the Father gives us, God's embrace, accepted and received by us with love. And we can take what we have done for others. Take care not to place your hope in money or pride, power or vanity, because they can promise you nothing good!

General audience, 11 June 2014

Vanity of vanities

'Vanity of vanities! All is vanity!' (*Eccles.* 1:2). Young people are particularly sensitive to the empty, meaningless values that often surround them. Unfortunately, moreover, it is they who suffer the consequences. Instead the encounter with the living Christ in his great family which is the Church fills hearts with joy, for it fills them with true life, with a profound goodness that endures, that does not tarnish. We saw it on the faces of the youth in Rio. But this experience must confront the daily vanity, that poison of emptiness that creeps into our society based on profit and possession and on consumerism and that deceives young people. This Sunday's Gospel reminds us, precisely, of the absurdity of basing our own happiness on having. The rich say to themselves: my soul, you have many possessions at your disposal . . . rest, eat, drink and be merry! But God says to them: Fools! This very night your life will be required of you. And all the things you have accumulated, whose will they be? (cf. *Lk* 12:19–20).

Dear brothers and sisters, the true treasure is the love of God shared with our brethren. That love which comes from

God and enables us to share it with one another and to help each other. Those who experience it do not fear death and their hearts are at peace.

Angelus, 4 August 2013

————

What is the kingdom of heaven?

But what is this kingdom of God, this *kingdom of heaven?* They are synonymous. We think immediately of the afterlife: eternal life. Of course this is true, the kingdom of God will extend without limit beyond earthly life, but the good news that Jesus brings us – and that John predicts – is that we do not need to wait for the kingdom of God in the future: it is at hand. In some way it is already present and we may experience spiritual power from now on. 'The kingdom of God is in your midst!', Jesus will say. God comes to establish his lordship in our history, today, every day, in our life; and there – where it is welcomed with faith and humility – love, joy and peace blossom.

Angelus, 4 December 2016

————

We will be like angels

In this world we live a provisional reality, which ends; conversely, in the afterlife, we will no longer have death as the horizon and will experience all things, even human bonds, in the dimension of God, in a transfigured way. Even marriage, a sign and instrument of God in this world, will shine brightly, transformed in the full light of the glorious communion of saints in paradise.

The 'sons of heaven and of the resurrection' are not a few privileged ones, but are all men and all women, because the salvation that Jesus brings is for each one of us. And the life of the risen shall be equal to that of angels (cf. *Lk.* 20:36), meaning wholly immersed in the light of God, completely devoted to his praise, in an eternity filled with joy and peace. But pay heed! Resurrection is not only the fact of rising after death, but is a new genre of life which we already experience now; it is the victory over nothing that we can already anticipate. Resurrection is the foundation of the faith and of Christian hope!

Angelus, 6 November 2016

———

Your fulfilment will be in God himself

Job was in darkness. He was right at death's door. And in that moment of anguish, pain and suffering, Job proclaimed hope: 'For I know that my Redeemer lives, and at last he will stand upon the earth ... my eyes shall behold [him], and not another' (Job 19:25, 27). The commemoration of the dead has this twofold meaning. A sense of sorrow: a cemetery is sad, it reminds us of our loved ones who have passed on. It also reminds us of the future, of death.

But in this sadness, we bring flowers, as a sign of hope, and also, I might say, of celebration, but later on, not now. And sorrow is mingled with hope. Today, in this celebration, this is what we all feel: the memory of our loved ones, before their remains, and hope.

But we also feel that this hope helps us, because we too must make this journey. All of us must make this journey. Sooner or later, with more pain or less, but everyone must. However with the flower of hope, with that powerful thread that is anchored in the hereafter. Thus, the hope of resurrection still does not disappoint.

Jesus was the first to make this journey. We are following the journey that he made. And it was Jesus himself who opened the door: with his cross he opened the door of hope, he opened the door for us to enter where we will contemplate God. 'I know that my Redeemer lives, and at last he will stand upon the earth . . . I shall behold him, and not another, I shall. My eyes shall behold him, and not another'.

Homily, 2 November 2016

――――

Be a saint, wherever you are!

Some think that sanctity is to close your eyes and to look like a holy icon. No! This is not sanctity! Sanctity is something greater, deeper, which God gives us. Indeed, it is precisely in living with love and offering one's own Christian witness in everyday affairs that we are called to become saints. And each in the conditions and the state of life in which he or she finds him- or herself. But you are consecrated. Are you consecrated? – Be a saint by living out your donation and your ministry with joy. Are you married? – Be a saint by loving and taking care of your husband or your wife, as Christ did for the Church. Are you an unmarried baptized person? – Be a saint by carrying out your work with honesty and competence and by offering time in the service of your brothers and sisters. 'But, father, I work in a factory; I work as an accountant, only with numbers; you can't be a saint there . . .' 'Yes, yes you can! There, where you work, you can become a saint. God gives you the grace to become holy. God communicates himself to you'. Always, in every place, one can become a saint, that is, one can open oneself up to this grace, which works inside us and leads us to holiness. Are you a parent or a grandparent? – Be a saint by passionately teaching your children or grandchildren to know and to follow Jesus. And it takes so much patience to do this: to be a good parent, a good grandfather, a good mother, a good grandmother; it takes so much patience and with this patience comes holiness: by exercising patience. Are you a catechist, an educator or a volunteer? Be a saint by becoming a visible sign of God's love and of his presence alongside us. This is it: every state of life leads to holiness, always! In your home, on the street, at work, at church, in that moment and in your state of life, the path to sainthood has been opened. Don't be discouraged to pursue this path. It is God alone who gives us the grace. The Lord asks only this: that we be in communion with him and at the service of our brothers and sisters.

General audience, 19 November 2014

Who doesn't believe in the Resurrection?

Unfortunately, efforts have often been made to blur faith in the Resurrection of Jesus and doubts have crept in, even among believers. It is a little like that 'rosewater' faith, as we say; it is not a strong faith. And this is due to superficiality and sometimes to indifference, busy as we are with a thousand things considered more important than faith, or because we have a view of life that is solely horizontal. However, it is the Resurrection itself that opens us to greater hope, for it opens our life and the life of the world to the eternal future of God, to full happiness, to the certainty that evil, sin and death may be overcome. And this leads to living daily situations with greater trust, to facing them with courage and determination. Christ's Resurrection illuminates these everyday situations with a new light. The Resurrection of Christ is our strength!

General audience, 3 April 2013

Walk towards the door!

It is a helmet. This is what Christian hope is. When we speak about hope we can be led to interpret it according to the common meaning of the term, that is, in reference to something beautiful that we desire, but which may or may not be attained. We hope it will happen; it is as a desire. People say, for example: 'I hope there will be good weather tomorrow!', but we know that there might be bad weather the following day . . . Christian hope is not like this. Christian hope is the expectation of something that has already been fulfilled; the door is there, and I hope to reach the door. What do I have to do? Walk towards the door! I am certain that I will reach the door. This is how Christian hope is: having the certainty that I am walking towards something that is, not something that I hope may be.

General audience, 1 February 2017

We will all be there together

We know from the Book of Revelation that God is preparing a new dwelling place and a new earth where justice will abide, and whose blessedness will answer and surpass all the longings for peace which spring up in the human heart' (*Lumen gentium*, 39). This is the Church's destination: it is, as the Bible says, the 'new Jerusalem', 'paradise'. More than a place, it is a 'state' of soul in which our deepest hopes are fulfilled in superabundance and our being, as creatures and as children of God, reach their full maturity. We will finally be clothed in the joy, peace and love of God, completely, without any limit, and we will come face to face with him!

(cf. *1 Cor* 13:12). It is beautiful to think of this, to think of heaven. We will all be there together. It is beautiful, it gives strength to the soul.

General audience, 26 November 2014

———

The slowness of the kingdom

Choosing God and his kingdom does not always immediately bear fruit. It is a decision one takes in hope and which leaves the complete fulfilment to God. Christian hope is extended to the future fulfilment of God's promise and does not stop in the face of difficulty, because it is founded on God's faithfulness, which never fails. He is steadfast; he is a faithful father; he is a faithful friend; he is a faithful ally.

Angelus, 26 February 2017

———

Only the poor really know how to hope

When a woman realizes she is pregnant, every day she learns to live in the expectation of seeing the gaze of that child that is to come. In this way too, we must live and learn from these human expectations and live in the expectation of seeing the Lord, of encountering the Lord. This is not easy, but we can learn: to live in expectation. To hope means and entails a humble heart, a poor heart. Only a poor man knows how to wait. Those who are already full of themselves and of their achievements are not able to place their trust in anyone other than themselves.

General audience, 1 February 2017

———

Don't allow the lamp of hope to burn out

Christian hope is not simply a desire, a wish, it is not optimism: for a Christian, hope is expectation, fervent expectation, impassioned by the ultimate and definitive fulfilment of a mystery, the mystery of God's love, in which we are born again and which we are already experiencing. And it is the expectation of someone who is coming: it is Christ the Lord approaching ever closer to us, day by day, and who comes to bring us at last into the fullness of his communion and of his peace. The Church then, has the task of keeping the lamp of hope burning and clearly visible, so that it may continue to shine as a sure sign of salvation and illuminate for all humanity the path that leads to the encounter with the merciful face of God.

General audience, 15 October 2014

———

Be a sign that anticipates the joys of heaven

The firm conviction of being loved by God is at the centre of your vocation: to be, for others, a tangible sign of the presence of God's kingdom, a foretaste of the eternal joys of heaven. Only if our witness is joyful will we attract men and women to Christ. And this joy is a gift that is nourished by a life of prayer, meditation on the word of God, the celebration of the sacraments and life in community, which is very important. When these are lacking, weaknesses and difficulties will emerge to dampen the joy we knew so well at the beginning of our journey.

Address, 16 August 2014

———

You are in his hands

Remaining firm in the Lord, in this certainty that he does not abandon us, walking in hope, working to build a better world, despite the difficulties and sad circumstances that mark our personal and collective existence, is what really counts; it is how the Christian community is called to encounter the day of the Lord.

In the Gospel Jesus encourages us to keep firmly in mind and in heart the certainty that God guides our history, and that he knows the final end of things and events. Under the Lord's merciful gaze, history unravels in flowing uncertainty, and weaves between good and evil. However, all that happens is contained within him; our lives cannot be lost because they are in his hands.

Angelus, 13 November 2016

For the Christian there is no distinction between who is dead and who is not, but between who is in Christ and who is not

It is good to grasp the kind of continuity and deep communion there is between the Church in heaven and that which is still a pilgrim on earth. Those who already live in the sight of God can indeed sustain us and intercede for us, pray for us. On the other hand, we too are always invited to offer up good works, prayer and the Eucharist itself in order to alleviate the tribulation of souls still awaiting never-ending beatitude. Yes, because from the Christian perspective the distinction is not between who is dead and who is not, but between who is in Christ and who is not! This is the point of determination, what is truly decisive for our salvation and for our happiness.

General audience, 26 November 2014

―――――

What awaits us?

This vision of heaven we just have heard described in the First Reading is very beautiful: the Lord God, beauty, goodness, truth, tenderness, love in its fullness. All of this awaits us. Those who have gone before us and who have died in the Lord are there. They proclaim that they have been saved not through their own works, though good works they surely did, but that they have been saved by the Lord: 'Salvation belongs to our God who sits upon the throne, and to the Lamb!' (*Rev*

7:10). It is he who saves us, it is he who at the end of our lives takes us by the hand like a father, precisely to that heaven where our ancestors are. One of the elders asks: 'Who are these, clothed in white robes, and whence have they come?' (v. 13). Who are these righteous ones, these saints who are in heaven? The reply is: 'These are they who have come out of the great tribulation; they have washed their robes and made them white in the blood of the Lamb' (v. 14).

We can enter heaven only thanks to the blood of the Lamb, thanks to the blood of Christ. Christ's own blood has justified us, which has opened for us the gates of heaven. And if today we remember our brothers and sisters who have gone before us in life and are in heaven, it is because they have been washed in the blood of Christ. This is our hope: the hope of Christ's blood! It is a hope that does not disappoint. If we walk with the Lord in life, he will never disappoint us!

Homily, 1 November 2015

Let us wait for the groom!

Dear brothers and sisters, here then is what we are awaiting: Jesus' return! The Church as bride awaits her groom! We must, however, ask ourselves with total sincerity: are we truly luminous and credible witnesses to this expectation, to this hope? Do our communities still live in the sign of the presence of the Lord Jesus and in the warm expectation of his coming, or do they appear tired, sluggish, weighed down by fatigue and resignation? Do we too run the risk of exhausting the oil of faith, and the oil of joy? Let us be careful!

General audience, 15 October 2014

———

Let each of your deeds be a seed that blossoms in God's garden

Were there no reference to paradise and to eternal life, Christianity would be reduced to ethics, to a philosophy of life. Instead, the message of Christian faith comes from heaven, it is revealed by God and goes beyond this world. Belief in resurrection is essential in order that our every act of Christian love not be ephemeral and an end in itself, but may become a seed destined to blossom in the garden of God, and to produce the fruit of eternal life.

May the Virgin Mary, Queen of heaven and earth, confirm us in the hope of resurrection and help us to make fruitful in good works her Son's word sown in our hearts.

Angelus, 6 November 2016

———

Everything is transformed, and your joy will be overflowing

Everything is transformed: the desert blooms, comfort and joy permeate hearts (cf. Is. 35: 5–6). These signs proclaimed by Isaiah as signs of salvation that is already present; they are fulfilled in Jesus. He himself affirms it by responding to the messengers sent by John the Baptist – what does Jesus say to these messengers? 'The blind receive their sight and the lame walk, lepers are cleansed and the deaf hear, and the dead are raised up' (*Mt* 11:5). They are not words, but are facts that demonstrate how salvation, brought by Jesus, seizes the human being and regenerates him. God has entered history to free us from the slavery of sin; he set his tent in our midst in order to share our existence, to heal our lesions, to bind our wounds and to give us new life. Joy is the fruit of this intervention of God's salvation and love.

We are called to let ourselves be drawn in by the feeling of exultation. This exultation, this joy ... But a Christian who isn't joyful is a Christian who is lacking something, or else is not a Christian! It is heartfelt joy, the joy within which leads us forth and gives us courage. The Lord comes, he comes into our life as a liberator; he comes to free us from all forms of interior and exterior slavery. It is he who shows us the path of faithfulness, of patience and of perseverance because, upon his return, our joy will be overflowing.

Angelus, 11 December 2016

––––––

The 'rule of life' of the believer who longs for God

A holy longing for God wells up in the heart of believers because they know that the Gospel is not an event of the past but of the present. A holy longing for God helps us keep alert in the face of every attempt to reduce and impoverish our life. A holy longing for God is the memory of faith, which rebels before all prophets of doom. That longing keeps hope alive in the community of believers, which from week to week continues to plead: 'Come, Lord Jesus'.

This same longing led the elderly Simeon to go up each day to the Temple, certain that his life would not end before he had held the Saviour in his arms. This longing led the Prodigal Son to abandon his self-destructive lifestyle and to seek his father's embrace. This was the longing felt by the shepherd who left the ninety-nine sheep in order to seek out the one that was lost. Mary Magdalene experienced the same longing on that Sunday morning when she ran to the tomb and met her risen Master.

Longing for God draws us out of our iron-clad isolation, which makes us think that nothing can change. Longing for God shatters our dreary routines and impels us to make the changes we want and need. Longing for God has its roots in the past yet does not remain there: it reaches out to the future. Believers who feel this longing are led by faith to seek God, as the Magi did, in the most distant corners of history, for they know that there the Lord awaits them.

Homily, 6 January 2017

————

You are clutching the anchor's rope

In the Second Reading, we heard what the Apostle John said to his disciples: 'See what love the Father has given us, that we should be called children of God; and so we are. The reason the world does not know us . . . We are God's children now; it does not yet appear what we shall be, but we know that when he appears we shall be like him, for we shall see him as he is' (1 Jn 3:1–2). To see God, to be like God: this is our hope. And today, on All Saints' Day and the first day that we commemorate the faithful departed, we need to think a little about this hope: this hope that accompanies us in life. The first Christians depicted hope with an anchor, as though life were an anchor cast on heaven's shores and all of us journeying to that shore, clinging to the anchor's rope. This is a beautiful image of hope: to have our hearts anchored there, where our beloved predecessors are, where the Saints are, where Jesus is, where God is. This is the hope that does not disappoint; today and tomorrow are days of hope.

Homily, 1 November 2015

PART IV

THOSE WHO PRAY
LEAD PEACEFUL LIVES

PRAYER COMPLETES
THE HUMAN BEING

'We must give space to the Spirit
so that it can advise us.
And giving space is praying, praying
that he will always come and help us.'

7 May 2014

———

Why Pope Francis is happy . . .

Q. (*boy*): Everyone in this world is trying to be happy. But we
have wondered: are you happy? If so, why?

A. (*Pope Francis*): Absolutely, absolutely, I am happy. And I am
happy because . . . I don't know why . . . perhaps because I
have a job, I'm not unemployed, I have a job, a job as a shepherd! I am happy because I found my path in life and
travelling that path makes me happy. And it is also a peaceful
happiness, because at that age it is not the same happiness as
a young person feels, there's a difference. A certain inner
peace, a great peace, a happiness that also comes with age.

And also with a path that has always had problems; even now there are problems, but that happiness doesn't go away with the problems, no: it sees the problems, suffers them and goes on; it does something to resolve them and goes on. But in the depths of the heart there is that peace and that happiness. It is a grace of God, for me, really. It is a grace. It is not a personal reward.

Interview with young people, 31 March 2014

There are as many ways of praying as there are people

How many different ways there are to pray for our neighbour! They are all valid and accepted by God if done from the heart. I am thinking in a particular way of the mothers and fathers who bless their children in the morning and in the evening. There is still this practice in some families: blessing a child is a prayer. I think of praying for sick people, when we go to visit them and pray for them; of silent intercession, at times tearful, in the many difficult situations that require prayer.

General audience, 30 November 2016

Pray with your works

Yesterday a good man, an entrepreneur, came to Mass at Santa Marta. That young man must close his factory because he cannot manage, and he wept, saying: 'I don't want to leave more than fifty families without work. I could declare the company bankrupt: I could go home with my money, but my heart would weep for these fifty families for the rest of my life'. This is a good Christian who prays through his works: he came to Mass to pray that the Lord give him a way out, not only for him but for the fifty families. This is a man who knows how to pray, with his heart and through his deeds, he knows how to pray for his neighbour. He is in a difficult situation, and he is not seeking the easiest way out: 'let them manage on their own'. This man is a Christian. It did me good to listen to him! Perhaps there are many like him today, at this time in which so many people are in difficulty because of a lack of work.

General audience, 30 November 2016

The true Christian prayer says: 'Father'

Jesus says that the Father who is in heaven 'knows what you need, even before you ask him'. 'Father'. That is the key of prayer. Without saying, without feeling that word inside you, you can't pray . . . Who am I praying to? Almighty God? It's too far away. I don't feel this and Jesus didn't feel it either. Who am I praying to? The cosmic God? That's a bit like habit these days, isn't it? Praying to the cosmic God. That polytheistic way of doing things that comes with a superficial culture.

You need to pray to 'our' Father, the one who made you, who gave you life, you, me . . . who travels your journey with you, who knows your whole life, all of it. Who knows what is good and what isn't so good. He knows everything . . . If we don't begin the prayer with that word, said not with the lips but with the heart, we can't pray like Christians.

Homily at the Chapel of Domus Sanctae Marthae, 20 June 2013

———

Let the Spirit pray within you

I also think of giving thanks for the good news about a friend, a relative, a co-worker: 'Thank you Lord, for this wonderful thing!' This too is praying for others! Thanking the Lord when things go well. At times, as Saint Paul says, 'we do not know how to pray as we ought, but the Spirit himself intercedes for us with sighs too deep for words' (*Rom* 8:26). It is the Spirit who prays in us. Therefore, let us open our heart, to enable the Holy Spirit, scrutinizing our deepest aspirations, to purify them and lead them to fulfillment. However, for us and for others, let us always ask that God's will be done, as in the *Our Father*, because his will is surely the greatest good, the goodness of a Father who never abandons us: pray and let the Holy Spirit pray in us. This is beautiful in life: to pray, thanking and praising the Lord, asking for something, weeping when there are difficulties, like that man. But let the heart always be open to the Spirit, that he may pray in us, with us and for us.

General audience, 30 November 2016

Pray to the Father of everyone and he loves everyone

Is God the Father of me alone? No, he is our Father, because I am not an only son. None of us is. If I can't be a brother, it would be difficult for me to become the son of this Father, because he is certainly my Father, but also a Father of others, of my brothers and sisters . . . If I am not at peace with my brothers, I can't call him Father. This explains how Jesus, having taught us the *Our Father*, immediately says: 'If you forgive others their sins, your Father in heaven will forgive you too; but if you don't forgive others, the Father won't forgive you your sins either'.

This is difficult. If it's difficult, it isn't easy. But Jesus has promised us the Holy Spirit. He is the one who teaches from within, from the heart, how to say 'Father' and how to say 'our', making peace with all our enemies.

Homily at the Chapel of Domus Sanctae Marthae, 20 June 2013

We make space with prayer

We always return to the same theme: prayer! Yet prayer is so important. To pray with the prayers that we all learned as children, but also to pray in our own words. To ask the Lord: 'Lord, help me, give me counsel, what must I do now?' And through prayer we make space so that the Spirit may come and help us in that moment, that he may counsel us on what we all must do. Prayer! Never forget prayer. Never! No one, no one realizes when we pray on the bus, on the road: we pray in the silence of our heart. Let us take advantage of these moments to pray, pray that the Spirit gives us the gift of counsel.

General audience, 7 May 2014

Learn what to say to the Lord

Jesus tells us: the Father knows things. Don't worry, the Father sends rain on the just and on sinners, the sun on the just and on sinners. From now on I would like everyone to pick up the Bible for five minutes during the day, and slowly recite Psalm 103: 'Praise the Lord, O my soul; all my inmost being, praise his holy name. Praise the Lord, O my soul, and forget not all his benefits – who forgives all your sins and heals all your diseases, who redeems your life from the pit and crowns you with love and compassion'. Pray the whole Psalm to him. And by doing this we will learn the things we must say to the Lord, when we ask him for his grace.

Homily at the Chapel of Domus Sanctae Marthae, 1 July 2013

Not what pleases me, but what pleases him

In intimacy with God and in listening to his Word, little by little we put aside our own way of thinking, which is most often dictated by our closures, by our prejudice and by our ambitions, and we learn instead to ask the Lord: what is your desire? What is your will? What pleases you? In this way a *deep, almost connatural harmony* in the Spirit grows and develops within us and we experience how true the words of Jesus are that are reported in the Gospel of Matthew: 'do not be anxious how you are to speak or what you are to say; for what you are to say will be given to you in that hour; for it is not you who speak but the spirit of your Father speaking through you' (10:19–20). It is the Spirit who counsels us, but we have to make room for the Spirit, so that he may counsel us. And to give space is to pray, to pray that he come and help us always.

General audience, 7 May 2014

Families that pray together

I would like to ask you, dear families: do you pray together from time to time as a family? Some of you do, I know. But so many people say to me: but how can we? As the tax collector does, it is clear: humbly, before God. Each one, with humility, allowing themselves to be gazed upon by the Lord and imploring his goodness, that he may visit us. But in the family how is this done? After all, prayer seems to be something personal, and besides there is never a good time, a moment of peace . . . Yes, all that is true enough, but it is also a matter of humility, of realizing that we need God, like the tax collector! And all families, we need God: all of us! We need his help, his strength, his blessing, his mercy, his forgiveness. And we need simplicity to pray as a family:

simplicity is necessary! Praying the *Our Father* together, around the table, is not something extraordinary: it's easy. And praying the Rosary together, as a family, is very beautiful and a source of great strength! And also praying for one another! The husband for his wife, the wife for her husband, both together for their children, the children for their grandparents . . . praying for each other. This is what it means to pray in the family and it is what makes the family strong: prayer.

Homily, 22 October 2013

POPE FRANCIS' PRAYERS
FOR A FULFILLED LIFE

'I don't know, perhaps it sounds bad,
but to some extent praying means annoying God
to make him listen to us.'

6 December 2013

———

The prayer of the sons and daughters, taught by Jesus:

Our Father in heaven,
hallowed be your name,
your kingdom come,
your will be done,
on earth as it is in heaven.
Give us today our daily bread.
And forgive us our debts,
as we also have forgiven our debtors.
And lead us not into temptation
but deliver us from the evil one.

The Psalm of the joy of those who have found fulfilment

(quoted by Pope Francis at the beginning of *Amoris Laetitia*)

Blessed are all who fear the Lord,
    who walk in obedience to him.
You will eat the fruit of your labour;
    blessings and prosperity will be yours.
Your wife will be like a fruitful vine
    within your house;
your children will be like olive shoots
    around your table.
Yes, this will be the blessing
    for the man who fears the Lord.
May the Lord bless you from Zion;
    may you see the prosperity of Jerusalem
    all the days of your life.
May you live to see your children's children –
    peace be on Israel.

Psalm 128:1–6

———

The psalm of those who want to learn what to ask of God

(Pope Francis invites you to read it slowly every day) (See Homily at the Chapel of Domus Sanctae Marthae, quoted on page 224)

Praise the Lord, my soul;
   all my inmost being, praise his holy name.
Praise the Lord, my soul,
   and forget not all his benefits –
who forgives all your sins
   and heals all your diseases,
who redeems your life from the pit
   and crowns you with love and compassion,
who satisfies your desires with good things
   so that your youth is renewed like the eagle's.

The Lord works righteousness
   and justice for all the oppressed.
He made known his ways to Moses,
   his deeds to the people of Israel:
The Lord is compassionate and gracious,
   slow to anger, abounding in love.
He will not always accuse,
   nor will he harbour his anger forever;
he does not treat us as our sins deserve
   or repay us according to our iniquities.
For as high as the heavens are above the earth,
   so great is his love for those who fear him;
as far as the east is from the west,
   so far has he removed our transgressions from us.

As a father has compassion on his children,
   so the Lord has compassion on those who fear him;
for he knows how we are formed,
   he remembers that we are dust.
The life of mortals is like grass,
   they flourish like a flower of the field;
the wind blows over it and it is gone,
   and its place remembers it no more.
But from everlasting to everlasting
   the Lord's love is with those who fear him,
   and his righteousness with their children's children –
with those who keep his covenant
   and remember to obey his precepts.

The Lord has established his throne in heaven,
   and his kingdom rules over all.

Praise the Lord, you his angels,
   you mighty ones who do his bidding,
   who obey his word.
Praise the Lord, all his heavenly hosts,
   you his servants who do his will.
Praise the Lord, all his works
   everywhere in his dominion.
Praise the Lord, my soul.

Psalm 103

Prayer of those who want to come back

Lord,
I have let myself be deceived,
in a thousand ways I have shunned your love
yet here I am once more
to renew my covenant with you.
I need you.
Save me once again, Lord,
take me once more into your redeeming embrace.

Evangelii gaudium

———

Thank you, O Holy Mother of the Son of God, Holy
Mother of God!
Thank you for your humility
which drew the gaze of God;
thank you for the faith with which you received his Word;
thank you for the courage with which you said 'Here I am',
forgetting yourself, enthralled by Holy Love,
made wholly one with his hope.
Thank you, O Holy Mother of God!
Pray for us, pilgrims in time;
help us to walk on the path of peace.
Amen.

Angelus, 1 January 2017

Sustain, Mother, the trusting expectation of our hearts

Mary, our Mother,
in Christ you welcome each of us as a son or daughter.
Sustain the trusting expectation of our hearts,
succour us in our infirmities and sufferings,
and guide us to Christ, your Son and our brother.
Help us to entrust ourselves to the Father who accomplishes great things.

Message for the World Day of the Sick, 2017

———

For the vocations of happy women and men

Father of mercy,
who gave your Son for our salvation
and who strengthens us always with the gifts of your Spirit,
grant us Christian communities which are alive, fervent and
  joyous,
which are fonts of fraternal life,
and which nurture in the young the desire to consecrate
  themselves
to you and to the work of evangelization.
Sustain these communities in their commitment
to offer appropriate vocational catechesis
and ways of proceeding towards each one's particular
  consecration.
Grant the wisdom

needed for vocational discernment,
so that in all things
the greatness of your merciful love may shine forth.
May Mary, Mother and guide of Jesus,
intercede for each Christian community,
so that, made fruitful by the Holy Spirit,
it may be a source of true vocations
for the service of the holy People of God.

Message for the World Day for Vocations, 2016

———

When we present ourselves to you

(Prayer for the dead by Father Antonio Rungi, recited by Pope Francis during the *Angelus*)

God of infinite mercy,
we entrust to your immense goodness
all those who have left this world for eternity,
where you wait for all humanity,
redeemed by the precious blood of Christ your Son,
who died as a ransom for our sins.

Look not, O Lord, on our poverty,
our suffering, our human weakness,
when we appear before you
to be judged for joy or for condemnation.
Look upon us with mercy,

born of the tenderness of your heart,
and help us to walk
in the ways of complete purification.
Let none of your children be lost
in the eternal fire,
where there can be no repentance.
We entrust to you, O Lord,
the souls of our beloved dead,
of those who have died
without the comfort of the sacraments,
or who have not had an opportunity to repent,
even at the end of their lives.

May none of them be afraid to meet You,
after their earthly pilgrimage,
but may they always hope to be welcomed
in the embrace of your infinite mercy.
May our Sister, corporal death, find us always vigilant in
     prayer
and filled with the goodness done in the course of our
     short
or long lives.
Lord, may no earthly thing ever separate us from You,
but may everyone and everything support us
with a burning desire to rest peacefully
and eternally in You.
Amen.

2 November 2014

Invocation of the man of peace
Lord God of peace, hear our prayer!

We have tried so many times and over so many years to resolve our conflicts by our own powers and by the force of our arms. How many moments of hostility and darkness have we experienced; how much blood has been shed; how many lives have been shattered; how many hopes have been buried . . . But our efforts have been in vain.

Now, Lord, come to our aid! Grant us peace, teach us peace; guide our steps in the way of peace. Open our eyes and our hearts, and give us the courage to say: 'Never again war!'; 'With war everything is lost'. Instil in our hearts the courage to take concrete steps to achieve peace.

Lord, God of Abraham, God of the Prophets, God of Love, you created us and you call us to live as brothers and sisters. Give us the strength daily to be instruments of peace; enable us to see everyone who crosses our path as our brother or sister. Make us sensitive to the plea of our citizens who entreat us to turn our weapons of war into implements of peace, our trepidation into confident trust, and our quarreling into forgiveness.

Keep alive within us the flame of hope, so that with patience and perseverance we may opt for dialogue and reconciliation. In this way may peace triumph at last, and may the words 'division', 'hatred' and 'war' be banished from the heart of every man and woman. Lord, defuse the violence of our tongues and our hands. Renew our hearts and minds, so that the word that

always brings us together will be 'brother', and our way of life
will always be that of: Shalom, Peace, Salaam!

Invocation for peace, 8 June 2014

_____

Mary, the woman of listening

Mary, woman of listening,
open our ears;
grant us to know how to listen to the word
of your Son Jesus among the thousands of words of this world;
grant that we may listen to the reality in which we live,
to every person we encounter,
especially those who are poor, in need, in hardship.

   Mary, woman of decision,
illuminate our mind and our heart,
so that we may obey, unhesitating,
the word of your Son Jesus;
give us the courage to decide,
not to let ourselves be dragged along,
letting others direct our life.

   Mary, woman of action,
obtain that our hands and feet move 'with haste' towards
   others,
to bring them the charity and love of your Son Jesus,
to bring the light of the Gospel to the world,
as you did. Amen.

Homily, 31 May 2013

For communities and vocations consecrated in the Church

Father of mercy,
who gave your Son for our salvation
and who strengthens us always with the gifts of your Spirit,
grant us Christian communities which are alive, fervent and
    joyous,
which are fonts of fraternal life, and which nurture in the
    young
the desire to consecrate themselves to you and to the work
    of evangelization.
Sustain these communities in their commitment
to offer appropriate vocational catechesis
and ways of proceeding towards each one's particular
    consecration.
Grant the wisdom
needed for vocational discernment,
so that in all things the greatness
of your merciful love may shine forth.
May Mary, Mother and guide of Jesus,
intercede for each Christian community,
so that, made fruitful by the Holy Spirit,
it may be a source of true vocations
for the service of the holy People of God.

Message, 29 November 2015

Prayer of Holy Thursday for priests

On this Holy Thursday, I ask the Lord Jesus to enable many
young people to discover that burning zeal which joy kindles
in our hearts as soon as we have the stroke of boldness
needed to respond willingly to his call.

On this Holy Thursday, I ask the Lord Jesus to preserve
the joy sparkling in the eyes of the recently ordained who go
forth to devour the world, to spend themselves fully in the
midst of God's faithful people, rejoicing as they prepare their
first homily, their first Mass, their first Baptism, their first
Confession . . . It is the joy of being able to share with
wonder, and for the first time as God's anointed, the treasure
of the Gospel and to feel the faithful people anointing you
again and in yet another way: by their requests, by bowing
their heads for your blessing, by taking your hands, by bringing you their children, by pleading for their sick . . .

Preserve, Lord,
in your young priests
the joy of going forth,
of doing everything as if for the first time,
the joy of spending their lives fully for you.

On this Thursday of the priesthood, I ask the Lord Jesus to
confirm the priestly joy of those who have already ministered
for some years. The joy which, without leaving their eyes, is
also found on the shoulders of those who bear the burden of

the ministry, those priests who, having experienced the labours of the apostolate, gather their strength and rearm themselves: 'get a second wind', as the athletes say.

Lord, preserve
the depth, wisdom and maturity
of the joy felt by these older priests.
May they be able to pray with Nehemiah:
'the joy of the Lord is my strength' (cf. *Neh* 8:10).

Finally, on this Thursday of the priesthood, I ask the Lord Jesus to make better known the joy of elderly priests, whether healthy or infirm. It is the joy of the cross, which springs from the knowledge that we possess an imperishable treasure in perishable earthen vessels. May these priests find happiness wherever they are; may they experience already, in the passage of the years, a taste of eternity (Romano Guardini).

May they know, Lord,
the joy of handing on the torch,
the joy of seeing new generations of their spiritual children,
and of hailing the promises from afar,
smiling and at peace, in that hope which does not disappoint.

Homily, 17 April 2014

Prayer to the Virgin to transform our hearts

Mary, Virgin and Mother,
you who, moved by the Holy Spirit,
welcomed the word of life
in the depths of your humble faith:
as you gave yourself completely to the Eternal One,
help us to say our own 'yes'
to the urgent call, as pressing as ever,
to proclaim the good news of Jesus.
Filled with Christ's presence,
you brought joy to John the Baptist,
making him exult in the womb of his mother.
Brimming over with joy,
you sang of the great things done by God.
Standing at the foot of the cross
with unyielding faith,
you received the joyful comfort of the resurrection,
and joined the disciples in awaiting the Spirit
so that the evangelizing Church might be born.
Obtain for us now a new ardour born of the resurrection,
that we may bring to all the Gospel of life
which triumphs over death.
Give us a holy courage to seek new paths,
that the gift of unfading beauty
may reach every man and woman.
Virgin of listening and contemplation,

Mother of love, Bride of the eternal wedding feast,
pray for the Church, whose pure icon you are,
that she may never be closed in on herself
or lose her passion for establishing God's kingdom.
Star of the new evangelization,
help us to bear radiant witness to communion,
service, ardent and generous faith,
justice and love of the poor,
that the joy of the Gospel
may reach to the ends of the earth,
illuminating even the fringes of our world.
Mother of the living Gospel,
wellspring of happiness for God's little ones,
pray for us.
Amen. Alleluia!

Evangelii gaudium, 288

Prayer of Saint Faustina

(which Pope Francis invited everyone to recite in the Message for World Youth Day 2016)

Help me, O Lord, that my eyes may be merciful, so that I may never suspect or judge from appearances, but look for what is beautiful in my neighbours' souls and come to their rescue.

Help me, that my ears may be merciful, so that I may give
heed to my neighbours' needs and not be indifferent to
their pains and moanings.

Help me, O Lord, that my tongue may be merciful, so that
I should never speak negatively of my neighbour, but
have a word of comfort and forgiveness for all.

Help me, O Lord, that my hands may be merciful and filled
with good deeds, so that I may do only good to my
neighbours and take upon myself the more difficult and
toilsome tasks.

Help me, that my feet may be merciful, so that I may hurry
to assist my neighbour, overcoming my own fatigue and
weariness. My true rest is in the service of my neighbour.

Sister Faustina Kowalska, Diary, 163